# Synkrētic

The Journal of Indo-Pacific
Philosophy, Literature & Cultures

2022 / № 2

Synkrētic
The Journal of Indo-Pacific Philosophy, Literature & Cultures

ISSN 2653-4029

Editor: Daryl Morini
Deputy Editor: Christian Romuss
Associate Editor: Devon Turner

www.synkretic.com

General enquiries: enquiries@synkretic.com

Correspondence should be addressed to

  The Editor, Synkrētic Journal
  c/o Irukandji Media Pty Ltd
  Unit 9 204 Alice St
  Brisbane City Qld 4000
  AUSTRALIA

*Synkrētic* acknowledges the traditional custodians of the lands of Brisbane on which we work, the Turrbal and Jagera peoples.

Published in Australia by Irukandji Press, Brisbane.
Irukandji Press is a trade name of Irukandji Media Pty Ltd.

ISBN 978-0-6454980-0-4

Layout and editorial matter: © Irukandji Media Pty Ltd, 2022

Essays, responses, stories and notes: © retained by respective authors or their estates and (re)printed here with permission OR source is in the public domain.

The moral rights of the authors have been asserted.

All rights reserved. No part of this publication may be reproduced, stored in a retrieval system, or transmitted in any form by any means without the prior permission in writing of the Editor of Synkrētic.

Cover design and typesetting: Arthur Arek

## *Contributors*

Barahgurrie · Beemunny · Robert Bernasconi
Anna Ezekiel · Luis González Obregón
Karoline von Günderrode · Span Hanna
Peter Hippai · Hippitha · Soraj Hongladarom
Preciosa de Joya · Robert Koenig
Katie Langloh Parker · Eunah Lee
Georg Christoph Lichtenberg · Zach Lindsey
Robert Louden · Matah · Freya Matthews
Fritz Mauthner · Bano Qudsia · Masood A. Raja
Christian Romuss · Han Shan
Jane Singleton · Simon Swift · Tony La Viña
Thongchai Winichakul · Chunjie Zhang

# *Acknowledgments*

*Synkrētic* №2 (Jun. 2022) was a collaborative enterprise involving 24 past and modern writers and oral history sources from 9 countries across the region.

Contributors to this issue were based in Australia (10), China (1), French Polynesia (1), Hong Kong (1), Mexico (1), the Philippines (2), Switzerland (1), Thailand (1), and the United States of America (6).

*Synkrētic* warmly thanks all rights holders from around the world whose support made this issue possible, and especially the people and organisations listed below.

*Editions Haere Pō*
*Pakistaniaat* (ISSN 1948-6529)
*Journal of Letters* (ISSN 0125-4820)

# Erratum

*Synkrētic* №1 (Feb. 2022)

P. 145, fn. †: An incorrect version of Mary Rokonadravu's biographical note was used. It should read: 'Mary Rokonadravu won the 2015 Commonwealth Short Story Prize for the Pacific. She taught writing in correctional facilities for the University of the South Pacific. She lives in Suva, Fiji.'

In loving memory of
*Natasha Seaman*

# Contents

The case of the two Tahitians ... 1

ESSAYS

*Freya Mathews*
To know the world we need to 'walk the land' ... 13

*Soraj Hongladarom*
How is Thai philosophy possible? ... 26

RESPONSES  *Kant and the Tahitians*

*Robert Koenig*
A second birth in Tahiti ... 41

*Simon Swift*
Kant's critique of idealised Tahitians ... 47

*Robert Bernasconi*
The whitewashing of Kant ... 56

*Chunjie Zhang*
Tahiti in the European mind ... 62

*Eunah Lee*
The colour blindness of reason ... 68

*Robert Louden*
Kant's impure ethics ... 75

STORIES

*Bano Qudsia*
King Buzzard ... 83
    TRANSLATED BY *Masood A. Raja*

*Peter Hippai* et al.
Bahloo the moon ... 107

*Luis González Obregón*
The soldier who teleported from Manila to Mexico     117
    TRANSLATED BY *Zach Lindsey*

NOTES

*Karoline von Günderrode*
Muhammad's dream in the desert     133
    TRANSLATED BY *Anna Ezekiel*

*Georg Christoph Lichtenberg*
An onion with a thousand roots     145
    TRANSLATED BY *Christian Romuss*

*Fritz Mauthner*
The critique of language     148
    TRANSLATED BY *Christian Romuss*

*Preciosa de Joya*
An encounter with Father Ferriols     153

*Tony La Viña*
Fr Roque J. Ferriols, SJ (1924-2021)     158

*Thongchai Winichakul*
The silence of Thai history     164

*Han Shan*
Spurned by philosophers     170
    TRANSLATED BY *Span Hanna*

EDITORIAL

# The case of the two Tahitians

A philosopher who met a doctor, a carpenter, or a shoemaker in a bar would be at risk of believing she had much to teach them about the world and even their trades. The reason for this is simply mathematical: whereas the carpenter has only one claim to expertise, carpentry, the philosopher takes the whole of life as her canvas, which includes carpentry.

Fatally, then, our philosopher could not help but reserve the right, even if only in theory, to opine, analyse, or comment on each area of human knowledge. But even a right that only exists in theory must on occasion be used in practice if it is not to be lost. It is this tragic fact which seals our philosopher's demise. For, if goaded into it by one or two drinks too many, she is in mortal danger of making use of the right bestowed on her by the pre-Socratics. That is, to theorise on the politics of nurse-doctor relations, elocute on the æsthetic intricacies of the French dovetail, and deliver a stirring homily on the ethics of meat consumption to three silent patrons.

Such awkward encounters may explain why Tagalog, the Filipino national language, minted the image of the philosopher or *pilosopo* as a foolish babbler 'who argues lengthily, whether rightly or wrongly.'[1] And if we are honest, we must concede that the highest literary representation of this type of philosopher is that of Dr Pangloss in Voltaire's *Candide*. A character whose name literally means 'Dr All Tongue', who holds expertise in something called metaphysico-theologo-cosmolo-nigology, which no one understands and he least of all. But it would be unfair to subject all philosophers to Voltaire's biting caricature, all the more so because he is not above reproach. Perhaps a thinker who wrote 2,000 treatises, encyclopædias, pamphlets, poems and over 20,000 letters is not best placed to critique the loquaciousness of other philosophers. *Qui s'y frotte, s'y pique*, as they say.[2]

But it is not necessarily true that the worst trait of many philosophers is their inability to hold their tongues. Witness the great lineage of worshippers of silence from the Pythagoreans to the Cynics and the Buddhist, Hindu, Muslim, Christian and practically all ascetics. It should not surprise us that even across these great monastic traditions, vows of silence were a more rarefied and respected kind than the banal vow of chastity, reflecting the common fear of the spiritual dangers facing the idle babbler. Even a fool who keeps silent is considered wise. But for every Socrates, whose disciples while away his last hours before his execution while 'he talks, talks, talks',[3] there is one Han Shan, a Chinese Buddhist recluse who composed verses in silent contemplation, scorning men as he sat 'crosslegged, wild hair waving at the sky.'[4] Even the Stoics, an ancient Greek school not averse to speech, promoted the virtue of silence. As Seneca rightly notes in his play *Thyestes*, 'the art of silence is taught by life's many ills,'[5] and he himself used an 'eloquent silence' to get points across.[6]

Verbosity cannot, then, be the chief sin of the philosopher. No, it is not that it speaks much that marks out this curious creature, which trait it shares with every kind of the *Homo intellectualis* species. The historian as well as the literary critic, the novelist and the poet each talk, usually about themselves, and all just as tiresomely. The true mark of the philosopher is not their mellifluous tongue, but the enormity of their self-given task whose reach encircles the globe many times over. Philosophy is special for encompassing all of life. From the stars and moons, quarks and qualia, Thales' gods and olive press, Aristotle's *Archē* and Plato's forms, to Diogenes' experiment in biology, which reportedly killed him after he ate a raw polyp—no object, concept, or discipline can be beyond its reach. No natural limits can hem in its pretensions. So, we shouldn't be surprised to find in Plato's *Republic*, a canonical text, Socrates weighing in on the medical, carpentry, and shoemaking professions.[7] Nietzsche[8] and Heidegger[9] also philosophised with and on the carpenter's hammer, which need not imply any knowledge of how to actually wield one.

No item big or small can escape the grasping of all true philosophers, whose subject matter is not one particular thing but *all* things, with the concrete always put in service of some more or less universal and necessarily abstract theory. At least so it once was in the philosophical heyday of the Western European tradition from the 18th to the 19th centuries, which produced some of the boldest philosophical world-building of this kind. The chief of these thinkers was the famed Prussian son Immanuel Kant (1724-1804). Kant compared his *Critique of Pure Reason* to 'the first thoughts of Copernicus',[10] and declared his work 'an entire revolution' and anything before it 'a mere groping' in the dark.[11] A revolution—now that is expansive! Kant did not hesitate to tear apart the 'cobwebs' of other schools of thought and to mock them as jugglers.[12]

But all expansiveness is forgiven someone whose revered *Critique* not only achieved the 'momentous restructuring of the domain of philosophy,'[13] but which has been compared to a holy book for its revolutionary effect on human thought. The German poet Heinrich Heine (1797-1856) ironically compared it to the Bible, for if the latter exorcises demons, Kant's *Critique of Pure Reason* cures bad thoughts.[14] Heine is right to call Kant 'the arch-destroyer' of old ideas more violent than an executioner, and to describe his as 'destructive, world-annihilating thoughts.'[15] For if a thousand other philosophers, swollen with vanity, fell victim to the original sin of the discipline—the desire to know it all—Kant almost succeeded. Heine writes:

Not without reason, therefore, did he compare his philosophy to the method of Copernicus…So formerly reason, like the sun, moved round the universe of phenomena, and sought to throw light upon it. But Kant made reason, the sun, stand still, and the universe of phenomena now turns round, and is illuminated the moment it comes within the region of the intellectual orb.[16]

Having recentred the West's intellectual universe, Kant earned his place at its centre. This achievement could not but leave a mark on Kant's own character, and it is noteworthy that his ethics fuses honour-loving 'pagan' pride with the 'monk's virtue' of humility.[17] But the risk was great indeed for Kant, for in destroying old worlds and fashioning a whole new one, he reached the searing heights at which the sun melts man-made wings. And so, it was inevitable that the world-destroying mind of the Königsberg professor, who despite having never ventured out of town and seen a mountain could describe nebulæ,[18] would overreach by directing his theories at shores and peoples he had never seen.

In this issue of *Synkrētic*, we find Kant mired in a controversy about a subject as remote from Prussia as far-away galaxies in this pre-colonial era: the Tahitians. His few sources on this people consisted of travel writings, entries in James Cook's diary, and his conversations with sailors at the port of Königsberg.[19] But this did not stop Kant from proffering opinions, which six interviewees analyse variously in this issue, along the lines of Tahitians being a waste of space on their island if all they do is graze as happily as cows and sheep. Would it not have been better for them not to exist at all?[20] This is a clear case of philosophy's expansive instinct running wild.

In his interview, Simon Swift, Associate Professor of Modern English Literature at the University of Geneva, takes the reader through the personal backstory of Kant's remark, which was in part a settling of scores with his former student-turned-philosophy superstar J.G. Herder (1744-1803).[21] The University of California's Associate Professor of German Chunjie Zhang explores the surprisingly commonplace idealisation of Tahiti in 18th and 19th century European culture, which was imagined as a land of untrammelled personal, religious, and sexual freedoms. Zhang offers the counter-example of Georg Forster (1754-1794), who accompanied his father on one of Cook's voyages. Although charmed by Tahiti, his descriptions were 'a serious science' based on empirical, first-hand observation, unlike Kant's, which were based on hearsay.[22]

In these two contemporaries' minds we find two contrasting images. In Forster's, the Tahitian is an individual being with blood and flesh and opinions who, like the old Tahitian in Diderot's *Supplement*, can retort to the Western critic of his culture that 'our happiness you can but disturb.'[23] In Kant's mind, the Tahitian is an abstraction prior to all experience and an inconvenient one at that, which must be subordinated to higher and higher abstractions like a species, history, and humanity to gain the right to speak about his own happiness.[24]

These two images collided upon Forster's return from Tahiti, when he publicly attacked Kant, the world-destroying genius of the *Critique*, for refusing to be cowed by facts when it came to the Tahitians. Forster was incensed by Kant's theory of race which, as Thomas P. Saine writes, speculated 'that the true color of the natives of Tahiti and other South Pacific islands was not yet known with certainty, because there had not yet been a Tahitian born in Europe for the inspection of anthropologists.'[25] Influenced by British empiricism, Forster critiqued Kant for projecting his concept of race onto the Tahitians, and then purporting to find it 'in a place where it does not exist.'[26] Instead of Tahitians being brought to him as he wished, Kant may have benefitted more from joining Forster and visiting them on Cook's second voyage, as the Tahiti-based Robert Koenig wryly notes.[27]

Robert Bernasconi, Edwin Erle Sparks Professor of Philosophy and African American Studies at Pennsylvania State University, writes that 'Kant was provoked by Georg Forster's description of Tahiti as one of the happiest spots on the globe' because he imagined non-white races to be less industrious than Europeans. 'He viewed the happiness of the Tahitians as a product of the ease with which they were able to provide for themselves…their happiness was their downfall.'[28] Robert Louden, Distinguished Professor of Philosophy at the University of Southern Maine, also observes that Kant's critique of the Tahitians hinges on their happiness. Because they supposedly only go about enjoying themselves, Kant looks down on them for violating their duty to themselves, which in his view is to develop their talents and rational capacities.[29]

Eunah Lee, Assistant Professor of Philosophy at St. Joseph's University, also points to Kant's 'fundamental anti-hedonism' as one of the reasons underlying his attack on the Tahitians. 'For Kant, the goal of human life is not to idle in a happy state but to strive for perfection through labour, to be worthy of happiness.' Kant assumes that 'humanity will fully reach its perfection *as a species*, not as individual human beings,' which leads him to think that 'humanity will fully reach its highest stage by the European white, denying other non-white races this privilege.'[30] While there is a broad consensus among interviewees on characterising these ideas as racist, the degree to which Kant's views reflected either prejudices widespread in his era or a central part of his philosophical project which served to justify later mass killings is still debated.

Beyond the black sand shores of French Polynesia, Issue 2 of *Synkrētic* takes the reader to Australia's Kakadu and Kimberley regions for a *tour d'horizon* of the Aboriginal concept of walking the land in Emeritus Professor Freya Matthews' page-turning essay.[31] This issue is also privileged to feature the ancient oral history of the Yuwaalaraay people from outback New South Wales, which tells the story of a lunar deity named Bahloo the moon.[32] With both focussing on Thailand, Professor Soraj Hongladarom of Chulalongkorn University takes readers inside the debate of how Thai philosophy is possible,[33] while the University of Wisconsin-Madison's Professor Emeritus Thongchai Winichakul shines a spotlight on the 6 October 1976 massacre in Bangkok.[34] And much as Zach Lindsey's charming new translation solves the centuries old mystery of a Spanish soldier who teleported from Manila to Mexico,[35] the reader is transported to inner-city Lahore by Masood A. Raja's scintillating translation of Pakistani writer Bano Qudsia's critically acclaimed novel *King Buzzard*.[36] This issue includes translations from the German—Anna Ezekiel's rendering of Karoline von Günderrode[37] and Christian Romuss' of Georg Lichtenberg and Fritz Mauthner[38]—and from the Chinese by Span Hanna.[39] Finally, Preciosa de Joya[40] and Tony La Viña[41] reflect on the life and teachings of the illustrious Filipino thinker Padre Roque (1924-2021).

*Synkrētic*

Each in their own way, these Indo-Pacific writers' thoughts and stories seek to portray their own cultural surroundings in intimately concrete detail before staking a claim to understanding the whole world, or some abstraction in its image. Philosophers of all traditions would do well to learn from their intellectual humility.

*Daryl Morini*

## Notes

1. Emerita Quito, cited in Anne Quito, 'The Philippines' greatest female philosopher', in *Synkrētic*, №1 (Feb. 2022): 116.
2. *Qui s'y frotte, s'y pique*: A French dictum first recorded in the 16th century meaning 'if you play with fire, you get burned'. Literally, 'rub it and you'll get stung,' with reference to the porcupine.
3. Lev Shestov, *All Things are Possible*, transl. S.S. Koteliansky (London: Martin Secker, 1920), 18, aphorism 5.
4. Han Shan, 'Spurned by philosophers', transl. Span Hanna, 171.
5. Seneca the Younger, *Thyestes*, line 317, in Allessandro Schiesaro, *The Passions in Play* (Cambridge: Cambridge University Press, 2003), 157.
6. Andreas Heil, 'Vision, Sound, and Silence in the "Drama of the World"', in *Brill's Companion to Seneca: Philosopher and Dramatist*, eds. Gregor Damschen and Andreas Heil (Leiden: Brill, 2014), 556.
7. Plato, *The Republic*, transl. C.D.C. Reeve (Indianapolis: Hackett, 2004), 53, 92, 113, 120, 142.
8. Friedrich Nietzsche, *Twilight of the Idols: Or, How to Philosophize with the Hammer*, transl. Richard Polt (Indianapolis: Hackett, 1997), 3.
9. David R. Cerbone, 'Composition and Constitution: Heidegger's Hammer', in *Philosophical Topics*, Vol. 27, No. 2 (Fall 1999): 309-329.
10. Immanuel Kant, *The Critique of Pure Reason*, transl. Paul Guyer and Allen W. Wood (Cambridge: Cambridge University Press, 1998), 110.
11. Kant, *The Critique of Pure Reason*, 113, 110.
12. Kant, *The Critique of Pure Reason*, 119, 200.
13. Jane Kneller, 'The Poem of the Understanding: Kant, Novalis, and Early German Romantic Philosophy', in *The Palgrave Handbook of German Romantic Philosophy*, ed. Elizabeth Millán Brusslan (London: Palgrave Macmillan, 2020), 22.

14  Heinrich Heine, *Religion and Philosophy in Germany: A Fragment* (London: Trübner & Co., Ludgate Hill, 1882), 107.
15  Heine, *Religion and Philosophy*, 109.
16  Heine, *Religion and Philosophy*, 114.
17  Robert B. Louden, 'Review: Kantian Moral Humility: Between Aristotle and Paul', in *Philosophy and Phenomenological Research*, Vol. 75, No. 3 (Nov. 2007), 632-633.
18  See 'Immanuel Kant: Discoverer of Nebulae and the Multi-galaxy Universe', in *Futurism*, 19 February 2014, available at: <https://futurism.com/kant>.
19  Chunjie Zhang, 'Tahiti in the European mind', 65.
20  'Does the author really mean that if the happy inhabitants of Tahiti, never visited by more cultured nations, had been destined to live for thousands of centuries in their tranquil indolence, one could give a satisfying answer to the question why they exist at all, and whether it would not have been just as good to have this island populated with happy sheep and cattle as with human beings who are happy merely enjoying themselves?' Immanuel Kant, 'Review of J. G. Herder's *Ideas for the philosophy of the history of humanity. Parts 1 and 2* (1785)', transl. Allen W. Wood, in Robert B. Louden and Günter Zöller (eds.), *Anthropology, History, and Education* (Cambridge: Cambridge University Press, 2007), 142.
21  Simon Swift, 'Kant's critique of idealised Tahitians', 47-55.
22  Chunjie Zhang, 'Tahiti in the European mind', 63.
23  Denis Diderot, 'Supplement to Bougainville's Voyage, 1772', transl. Carole Warman *et al.*, in *Tolerance: The Beacon of the Enlightenment* (Cambridge: Cambridge University Press, 2016), 114-115.
24  Robert Bernasconi, 'The whitewashing of Kant', 56-61.
25  Thomas P. Saine, *Georg Forster* (New York: Twayne Publishers, Inc., 1972), 45.
26  Saine, *Georg Forster*, 45.
27  Robert Koenig, 'Kant and the Tahitians', 44-45.
28  Robert Bernasconi, 'The whitewashing of Kant', 59.
29  Robert Louden, 'Kant's impure ethics', 77.
30  Eunah Lee, 'The colour blindness of reason', 71.
31  Freya Matthews, 'To know the world we need to "walk the land"', 13-25.
32  Peter Hippai *et al.*, 'Bahloo the moon', 107-116.
33  Soraj Hongladarom, 'How is Thai philosophy possible?', 26-40.
34  Thongchai Winichakul, 'The silence of Thai history', 164-169.
35  Luis González Obregón, 'The soldier who teleported from Manila to Mexico', transl. Zach Lindsey, 117-132.
36  Bano Qudsia, 'King Buzzard', transl. Masood A. Raja, 83-106.
37  Karoline von Günderrode, 'Muhammad's dream in the desert', transl. Anna Ezekiel, 133-144.

38  Georg Christoph Lichtenberg, 'An onion with a thousand roots', transl. Christian Romuss', 145-147; and Fritz Mauthner, 'The critique of language', transl. Christian Romuss, 148-152.
39  Han Shan, 'Spurned by philosophers', transl. Span Hanna, 170.
40  Preciosa de Joya, 'An encounter with Father Ferriols', 153-157.
41  Tony La Viña, '*Obituary*: Fr Roque J. Ferriols, SJ (1924-2021)', 158-163.

# ESSAYS

# To know the world we need to 'walk the land'*

*Freya Mathews*[†]

Let us begin where environmental philosophy, my own discipline, first began, with the problem of anthropocentrism, that long-standing condition of moral myopia with which Western thought has been historically afflicted. Anthropocentrism consists in seeing human beings as the sole locus of moral significance, the centre and exclusive compass of the moral universe. Let us approach this problem as a problem of knowledge, and consider whether it will be resolved simply by increased knowledge, and specifically by increased scientific understanding of the nature of living things.

In this connection it is worth noting that prevailing Western assumptions about the nature of living things do seem currently to be undergoing rather rapid transformation. The new ideas are moreover no longer just the province of activists, such as the young climate strikers, or of writers and artists, or of relatively marginal academic discourses, such as environmental philosophy itself and the environmental humanities more generally, or of religious trailblazers such as Pope Francis. They are also now emanating from what is epistemologically the very core and driver of modern civilisation, namely science itself.

---

[*] This essay is adapted from a longer article entitled 'Conservation needs a "story about feeling"', forthcoming in *Biological Conservation* in 2022.

[†] Freya Mathews FAHA is Emeritus Professor of Environmental Philosophy at La Trobe University. Professor Mathews holds a PhD from the University of London. She lives in Melbourne, Australia.

## To know the world we need to 'walk the land'

Recent developments in plant and animal sciences are opening windows into exciting new worlds of nonhuman intelligence and consciousness. Leading neuroscientists, for example, have declared that many species of animals possess the same basic neurological substrates that generate consciousness in humans. Neurology pertaining to emotions in particular is found in a wide range of species. Animals which are neurologically wired in this way must, these scientists insist, experience the same emotions and associated states of consciousness as humans, including fear, terror, jealousy, and grief. Even entomologists, such as eminent conservation scientist E.O. Wilson, describe certain species of ants and bees as literally learning from experience and making decisions.[1]

In recent years, a number of botanists have gone further still by ascribing mind, or at any rate mind-like properties, to plants and perhaps to fungi. We have all heard how trees in forests, for instance, communicate with one another via electrical and chemical signals transmitted through underground mycorrhizal networks.[2] Mature, healthy trees also deliver nutrients and water through these same networks to trees in need and can warn neighbours of imminent dangers such as insect attacks. In experiments, botanist Monica Gagliano has shown that plants can 'learn' to distinguish between relevant and irrelevant stimuli and will 'remember' what they have learned for extended periods.[3] Not all botanists agree with such interpretations of the experimental findings, but these interpretations are being widely discussed.

But will such scientific findings transform social attitudes towards the biosphere? Will they lead us out of the exploitative attitudes that are currently ravaging life on Earth? Will they, in other words, expand the moral horizons of the industrial world? Will acknowledging that the mental lives of animals, plants, and perhaps other life forms are on a par with our own mental lives induce us to embrace them as fellow beings as morally considerable in their own way as ourselves? Do these new sciences mark a turning point in our Western attitude to the natural world, a point at which we will give up our old anthropocentric habit of treating nature as a mere stockpile of resources and begin to see it instead as a vast and variegated manifold of mind that deserves to be treated with full respect?

If we rely *exclusively* on science as our ultimate 'reason to believe', as many industrialised and particularly Western societies do today, then perhaps not. Modern industrialised societies rely exclusively on science in the sense that, for them, science retains the ultimate authority in matters of ontology. Views about the nature of reality do not qualify as legitimate in such societies unless they are sanctioned by science. Those which diverge from science may be tolerated at a private level but will not be adopted as a basis for policy until they square with science. As long as science retains this authority as the ultimate arbiter of reality, societies will be likely to continue subordinating the rest of nature to human interests. They will, in other words, continue to suffer from the moral blindness of anthropocentrism because, despite the wonder and intellectual excitement occasioned by the new scientific findings on mind in nature, nature will still not register in these societies as emotionally salient. Or so I wish to argue here.

On what basis do I argue this? Why do I want to suggest that science will not only fail to change our moral orientation to the world but may even reinforce our present anthropocentric orientation? By way of answer, let us first dig down a little into this notion of 'moral orientation'. On the face of it, a consensus amongst scientists that animals and perhaps plants are aware of their environment and disposed to act purposively in relation to it would imply that they have ends and meanings of their own. They would therefore count as 'subjects of a life' or 'teleological centres of life', rather than mere mechanisms or objects.

If, as much moral philosophy suggests, being the subject of a life or a teleological centre of life rather than a mere object is a basis for moral attribution, it rationally follows that animals and plants ought indeed to be entitled to moral consideration.[4] And although many people, including scientists, might be prepared to concede all this in light of emerging scientific evidence, this rational stance might not be reflected in the way those people actually behave towards plants, animals, and ecological communities generally. A gap may persist between the way they act towards other people and the way they act towards members of non-human species. At the more inchoate level of lived consciousness—the level of consciousness at which cognition is thickly infused with emotion and desire—people may, in other words, despite their rational convictions, remain morally invested mainly in humans even while rationally conceding the moral considerability of non-human beings.

This disjunction between the "facts" discovered by science and our moral *orientation* to these "facts" arises, I would suggest, from science itself. It emanates from a distinction between what science reveals about the world "out there", which is to say the "facts", and the attitude it imposes on us as knowers in relation to these "facts". For in order to obtain the facts, we must pursue a method that involves, as its very first principle, a stance of neutrality. The scientific knower must step back and assume the viewpoint of a detached observer, setting aside not only his preconceptions but his own agency and any self-interested or emotional investment he may have in the phenomenon under investigation. This phenomenon—whether it be a rock, molecule, mouse, rainforest, or gravitational field—is to become, for the purposes of the inquiry, an object or domain of purely intellectual interest to him. His goal is to perceive it just as it is in itself, undistorted by his preconceptions or projections or indeed by any attempts of the object itself to influence his representation of it. This stance of detached neutrality is key to the guiding ideal of "objectivity" which is so characteristic of scientific knowledge and is the linchpin of its authority in society.

Let me elaborate just a little here on this stance of detached neutrality and how it is reflected in the scientific method. In order to ensure that this stance is achieved, and that the requirements of emotional and value neutrality are met, science imposes conditions on the kind of evidence that may be used in support of scientific theories. Such evidence must be empirical and in principle universally accessible. It should not, for example, be accessible only to persons with special, *e.g.* mystical or supernormal epistemic powers or faculties. Nor should it consist in inherently one-off occurrences. For the findings of one investigator must in principle be open to the scrutiny of others if subjective distortions in those findings are to be detectable.

In other words, the observations used to support a scientific claim must be *repeatable*. Other investigators, in different circumstances and of different backgrounds, must be able to make the same set of observations for themselves. This methodological requirement of repeatability in turn gives rise to a preference, within science, for the experimental method. By making observations within the controlled conditions of a laboratory, an investigator is more likely to be able to satisfy the requirement of repeatability than if she simply observed events in the field. For other investigators can in principle set up the same conditions in their own laboratories, thereby verifying or falsifying the first investigator's findings. In this way the scientific aim of achieving objectivity by eliminating subjective factors from the inquiry leads to certain, broad methodological norms that are basic to the self-understanding of science.[5]

In focussing here on the epistemic stance of detached neutrality in science, and the correlative norm of objectivity, I am not setting out to discredit science. In important respects this stance is valuable, inasmuch as it offers a rigorous antidote to epistemic bad faith—to the bad faith that consists in believing whatever one wishes to believe, in projecting onto the data one's own wishes, biases, personal interests, or ideological fantasies. In the political climate of irrationalism, 'alternative facts', spin, 'fake news', and general epistemic irresponsibility that is currently rampant in many parts of the world, the norm of scientific objectivity must surely be steadfastly defended.

At the same time, however, we need to recognise that detached neutrality as a basis of epistemology has a price: it cuts us off affectively from the "object" of our investigations. As a way of knowing, it distances us emotionally and psychically from the known by requiring that we separate ourselves from the object for the purposes of the investigation, seeing it as totally "other", in no way implicated in the fabric of our own existence. Only in this way, according to the assumptions shaping the epistemology of science, will it be possible for the knower to divest herself of subjective investments in the object that may distort her representation of it. Accordingly, regardless of whether or not her investigative findings show this "object" to be endowed with mind, as a scientist she will necessarily remain affectively removed from it, unmoved by it.

To point this out is not, of course, to say anything new. The ideal of objectivity in science has been critically debated from a variety of disciplinary perspectives over many decades. The part of this debate that I am picking up here is not the question of whether science can live up to its ideal of objectivity. Clearly it cannot live up to it fully, since there are values and aspirations built into the very project of science itself, and indeed into human cognition *per se*. But that is not my point here. For the purposes of the current argument I am content to allow that, through its distinctive methods, science can indeed achieve, to a significant degree, the form of objectivity to which it aspires. My point is rather to draw attention to the moral consequences of this way of knowing for the "objects" that science purports to know.

These consequences were brilliantly analysed by a whole school of feminist philosophers of science in the 1980s and 1990s. I do not have space in this essay to set out the details of this analysis.[6] Suffice it to say that for centuries, as this analysis has shown, the objectifying tendency inherent in scientific epistemology led it to construct nature literally as an object, one entirely devoid of mind, incapable of engaging intersubjectively with the knower. That is to say, the epistemology of science was subconsciously projected by scientists as ontology. Nature was understood to be nothing but an elaborate mechanism moved not by any inherent meaning and value, but only by cause and effect. Now, at last, science is starting to discard those old projective blinkers. It is discovering that the natural world is in fact full of minds—animal minds, plant minds, fungal minds, forest minds, and perhaps a Gaian mind. Exhilarating as this discovery is, however, it is still essentially a matter of merely intellectual interest, a division of science, part of a larger architectonic premised on affective detachment. As such, it is unable in the end to make animals,

*Synkrētic*

plants, fungi, or indeed anything emotionally or psychically salient to us.

This disconnect between scientific cognition and affective engagement is dramatically confirmed when we consider that the Cambridge Declaration on Animal Consciousness of 2012—the declaration by leading neuroscientists that many animal species share with humans the same basic range of emotional experience—has made no appreciable difference to the way science-based societies treat animals.[7] They continue to be systematically exploited and killed on an industrial scale to serve human interests.

Again, in making this point about science I am not denying that in a world of seven and a half billion people, science as a tool of economic production and environmental and climate repair remains indispensable. But if modern humanity is to become properly morally *invested* in the lives of other beings and larger life communities, it seems that something more than the kind of cognition involved in science is required. Those lives and communities must matter to us, and for them to matter to us we may need to complement science with other, more engaged ways of knowing.

What other, more engaged ways of knowing are there? This is, again, a question that may be explored from a variety of different philosophical perspectives. In an Australian context, however, one approach seems particularly salient. For in Australia we are of course lucky to have on hand teachers of supremely engaged ways of knowing—ways that intrinsically lead not only to detailed empirical knowledge of one's natural environment but to a sense of intimacy and connection with it. I am speaking about the ways of knowing described by many Aboriginal authorities.

In her deeply insightful book, *The Land is the Source of the Law*, Indigenous scholar Christine Black offers perceptive interpretations of texts by Senior Law Men (SLM) such as Bill Neidjie of Kakadu in northern Australia and David Mowaljarlai of the Kimberley in northwestern Australia, amongst others. As both these Senior Law Men emphasise, Aboriginal ways of knowing cannot be extricated from *feeling*. One arrives at such knowledge not by adopting the stance of a detached observer, but by, as Mowaljarlai puts it, 'walk-

*To know the world we need to 'walk the land'*

ing the land'—meaning not merely walking over the land, traversing it, but walking with it, entering it. Indeed, knowing in this way is not a matter of adopting a "stance" at all, of stepping out of the sphere of action to take up a "standpoint" from which the action can be passively watched; it is rather a matter of diving into that sphere, stepping into the midst of it, joining forces with it.[8]

Guided by the interpretations that Christine Black provides, I take SLM Mowaljarlai's phrase to mean that we should walk the land not merely in a literal sense but in a paradigm-shifting epistemological sense as well. Rather than stepping back from the land, we need actively to *address* it, engaging with it communicatively, both as a member of its community and as a collaborator with it in shared endeavours. Such community membership and collaboration will certainly require empirical attentiveness on our part—we will need to pay close attention to the dispositions and behaviours of everything around us and become alert to signals of social intent. We shall also need to be attuned to larger shifting patterns of circumstance and meaning. 'Walking the land' thus does call for powers of perception free of distorting filters, and in this sense it calls for a form of "objectivity" on our part. But, in this case, objectivity emanates not from detachment but from relationship: we seek to engage the land by interesting it in ourselves. We do this partly by opening ourselves communicatively to it, for example via ceremony, and partly by joining with it in shared ends—ends that serve its interests as well as our own. To be able to join with it in shared ends in this way, we must be able to identify those ends accurately, without prejudice. If we succeed by these means in slipping into relationship with the land, we may hope that it will respond to us in self-revelatory ways that will remain forever hidden to the detached observer. We may come to know it, in other words, far more deeply than the scientist can.

While SLM Mowaljarlai does not describe what it is like qualitatively to experience such responsiveness, a hint is provided by Frans Hoogland, associate of another Senior Law Man, Paddy Roe of the Kimberley, and an initiated Lawman himself. In the Kimberley, as Hoogland explains, there is a term for such attunement to the communicative aspect of country: *liyan*. This term signifies a visceral way of knowing through feeling that is shared not only by people but by all beings and by land itself. Frans, in dialogue with Paddy Roe, explains *liyan* as follows.

> In order to experience [this feeling], we have to walk the land. At a certain time for everybody, the land will take over. The land will take that person. You think you're following something, but the land is actually pulling you. When the land starts pulling you, you're not even aware you're walking—you're off, you're gone. When you experience this, it's like a shift of your reality. You start seeing things you never seen before…all of a sudden, [your old way of seeing] doesn't fit anything. Then something comes out of the land, guides you. It can be a tree, a rock, a face in the sand, a bird…Then another thing might grab your attention, and before you know it there's a path created that is connected to you. It belongs to you, and that is the way you start to communicate with the land, through your path experiences. And that path brings you right back to yourself. You become very aware about yourself. You start to tune finer and finer. Then you become aware that when you're walking the path, it's coming out of you—you are connected to it…[When this happens] we get a shift in mind that drops down to a feeling. Then we wake up to feeling, what we call *le-an* [*liyan*] here, and we become more alive, we start feeling, we become more sensitive. You start to read the country…Then you wake up…and the country starts living for you. Everything is based on that feeling *le-an* [*liyan*], seeing through that feeling.[9]

If I understand Hoogland aright, *liyan* is a faculty of cognitive feeling that allows one to sense the world as subtly opening or closing, according to circumstances, as one walks the land. This sensitivity is a matter of *feeling*, not only inasmuch as it is guided by intuitive, body-based awareness but also in a more affective sense. One leans into the openings or, in face of resistances, one steps back and adjusts one's behaviour, simply because it feels right, affectively speaking, to do so. It feels right to find oneself in a groove—to find oneself slipping into a yielding flow of circumstances; a groove which it would be discomfiting to resist.

In time, one may so develop this faculty of awareness that it informs one's daily dealings. Which direction should one take when one is walking on country? With whom should one associate on country? How should one comport oneself on country? One's feeling for country may come to guide one's steps, one's choices, in the most minute of particulars. To be accompanied by country in this way, to be in such mutually responsive moment-by-moment attunement with it, of course does not leave one unmoved. On the contrary, it may pierce one through and through, shifting one on one's metaphysical moorings, rearranging one's entire hierarchy of allegiances and loyalties.

To dwell consistently in such a state of attunement is to match a more general definition of *liyan* as the wellbeing that radiates from one's core when all of one's relationships—with country, community, culture, and oneself—are in balance.[10] Being in balance, in this context, might be understood as a state of existing and acting in tune with a deep inner "Ought", a "right way" which is not some contingent social convention but an alignment with a normative axis at the core of reality, a normative axis that is, in Aboriginal parlance, referred to as Law.[11] Because acting Lawfully is not acting out of "conscience" or "duty" but out of visceral feeling, which is both cognitive and affective, Law is self-validating and self-enforcing. It is not, as Western law is, a set of rules or conventions imposed on us from without and designed to thwart our will or restrain our inclination. It is rather, once we have developed a feeling for it, co-incident with our own deepest will.

Another research team based in the Kimberley summarises *liyan* as follows:

It is our moral compass, our intuition, which guides us through life. *Liyan* can teach us to feel and build our own relationship with Country. *Liyan* is our inner spirit, and when it connects with the spirit of Country it heightens our sense of wellbeing, of balance and harmony. Country has this *liyan* too, and it is reciprocal…We all have this capacity.[12]

As both Hoogland and Mowaljarlai emphasise, to awaken this faculty we have to walk the land, not merely in a recreational sense as hikers or tourists but in an agentic, addressive, collaborative sense. It was natural for Aboriginal people to walk the land in this way because they traditionally lived off it, and therefore needed to be intimately attuned to its affordances. By the same token, they needed to be accurately apprised of its interests in order to ensure,

*Synkrētic*

by means of a suite of highly skilled interventions, its continued ecological flourishing. Walking the land, in other words, was integral to their basic economic praxis.

But the praxis of modern industrialised societies, shaped as that praxis has been by the detached epistemology of science, is far removed from this two-way relationship with land. Everything we do in industrial societies—the entirety of our economic effort—reflects the detachment and hence the instrumentalism of the scientific attitude. Does it not follow, then, that as members of such societies we are locked into this attitude, and hence locked out of the moral experience of 'walking the land'? How can we possibly, as members of modern societies, recover the faculty of cognitive feeling, known in the Kimberley as *liyan*, that would reconnect us at the level of feeling to our natural environment, rendering its needs as transparent to us as our own?

In this essay I can only offer pointers towards an answer to this question, pointers which I have developed elsewhere.[13]

My first suggestion is that, although it is impossible for seven and a half billion people to return to the pre-industrial, in some cases even pre-agrarian, economic praxes of Aboriginal Australia, there might be other practices that could involve us as participants to some degree in the life of the land. I am thinking here of practices of private conservation. If people, individually or in small groups, routinely cared for land as part of their regular lives—through hands-on, *in situ*, on-the-ground practices such as planting, seeding, weeding, thinning, restoring soils, and selective burning—they would likely become intimately acquainted with the ecology of a particular place, not merely theoretically but corporeally. In consequence, they might become more attuned to the responses of that place to their efforts. Such a process, requiring sensitivity to both the pushback and the receptivity of land to one's interventions, would take time. But given time, one's eyes might gradually become opened. Once attentive to all the specific forms of life and being that arise in a particular locale, as well as to their interrelations, one might find oneself drawn into ever-deepening relationship with the ecosystem or ecosystems in question. The land might indeed begin to open to one, to come alive, and a whole new horizon of relationship, presence, communicativity, enthralment, mystery, and indeed revelation may come into view.

If this is to happen, however, it is vital that this very personal, hands-on practice of conservation be carried out in a particular place, and with continuity over the long term. It should preferably be practised over the term of one's entire life, so that genuine trust and rapport can develop. It may also have a better chance of success if the individual practitioner is part of a group of equally committed conservation practitioners, all caring for the same place, sharing their resources, discoveries, and insights. This would add an element of *affiliation* to the practice. Affiliation is surely key to human identity and will for this reason help to give the practice of conservation an existential force perhaps comparable, as a shaper of consciousness, to that of economic praxis. The practitioner's developing relationship with land will be extended into relationships with a congregation of fellow landkeepers, all with a sense of belonging to the same place. Finding one's way into such a close-knit terrain of relationships, not as a note-taking outsider but as a committed insider, might indeed in due course help to place one back *inside* the world, morally speaking, rather than leaving one stranded as a curious but neutral observer outside it.[14]

My second suggestion is that we could try to ensure that, in settler and other societies in which pre-industrial land traditions are still strong, those who are professionally responsible for the conservation of public lands are no longer trained exclusively in science. They could also be inducted into alternative local epistemologies by traditional knowledge-holders. I have described this elsewhere as a process of Indigenising conservation. If this were incorporated at an institutional level as an essential component of conservation education, we could expect to see profound moral shifts in conservation priorities and policies. These shifts might in turn be expected to have ripple effects on attitudes to the environment, and indeed to reality itself, throughout society.[15]

*Synkrētic*

## Notes

1. E.O. Wilson and Bert Hölldobler, *The Superorganism* (New York: W.W. Norton, 2009).
2. Peter Wohlleben, *The Hidden Life of Trees* (Munich: Ludwig Verlag, 2015).
3. Michael Pollan, 'The intelligent plant', in *The New Yorker*, 15 December 2013, available at: <https://www.newyorker.com/magazine/2013/12/23/the-intelligent-plant>.
4. Andrew Brennan and Norva Y.S. Lo, 'Environmental Ethics', in *The Stanford Encyclopedia of Philosophy* (Summer 2022 Edition), ed. Edward N. Zalta, forthcoming in: <https://plato.stanford.edu/archives/sum2022/entries/ethics-environmental/>.
5. Freya Mathews, 'To Know the World', in *On the Edge of Discovery: Australian Women in Science*, ed. Farley Kelly (Melbourne: Text Publishing, 1993), 199-227.
6. For an overview of this literature see Mathews, 'To Know the World' (1993).
7. See Jaak Panksepp, Diana Reiss, David Edelman, Bruno van Swinderen, Philip Low and Christof Koch, *The Cambridge Declaration on Consciousness*, 7 July 2012, in Cambridge, UK, available at: <https://fcmconference.org/img/CambridgeDeclarationOnConsciousness.pdf>.
8. C.F. Black, *The Land is the Source of the Law* (London: Routledge, 2010).
9. Jim Sinatra and Phin Murphy, *Listen to the People, Listen to the Land* (Melbourne: Melbourne University Press, 1999), 19-21.
10. Mandy Yap and Eunice Yu, 'Community well-being from the ground up: a Yawuru example', in *BCEC Research Report*, No. 3/16, August 2016.
11. Freya Mathews, 'From Wilderness Preservation to the Fight for Lawlands', in *Rethinking Wilderness and the Wild: Conflict, Conservation and Co-existence*, ed. Robyn Bartel *et al.* (New York: Routledge, 2020).
12. Sandra Wooltorton *et al.*, 'Becoming family with place', in *Resurgence and Ecologist*, Issue 322, (Sept./Oct. 2020): 34-35.
13. Freya Mathews '"Walking the Land": an Alternative to Discourse as a Path to Ecological Consciousness and Peace', in *Towards a Just and Ecologically Sustainable Peace*, eds. Joseph Camilleri and Deborah Guess (London: Palgrave Macmillan, 2020); Freya Mathews, 'Environmental struggles in Aboriginal homelands: Indigenising conservation', in *Journal of Human Rights and the Environment*, Vol. 12, Issue 1 (2021): 51-68.
14. Freya Mathews, 'Walking the Land' (2020).
15. Freya Mathews, 'Environmental struggles in Aboriginal homelands' (2021).

# How is Thai philosophy possible?*

*Soraj Hongladarom*†

## I. Why ask the question?

The relationship between the disciplines of philosophy and area studies seems to be tenuous. For one thing, philosophy is a normative discipline *par excellence*, while area studies is an empirical investigation aimed at gaining a detailed understanding of the area in question through observation and theory-making. This does not mean, however, that philosophy has absolutely no role to play, for area studies, being interdisciplinary in nature, has a tendency to include disciplines which can shed light on the main problems of the field. Its role, nonetheless, is usually limited to a kind of expository or explanatory investigation of the systems of thought or ways of thinking of the people in the area. That is not the same as philosophy, for if it were so, philosophy would be no different from intellectual history or cultural anthropology. And if philosophy cannot be distinguished from these disciplines then that would present a very strong case against keeping philosophy a viable discipline in this day and age. It seems that if philosophy cannot show anything

---

\* This paper was originally presented at the International Conference on Thai Studies, Chiang Mai University, 14 to 17 October 1996. It was first published in the *Journal of Letters*, Volume 43, Issue 1 (2016): 183-199. This lightly edited version is reprinted with the gracious permission of the *Journal of Letters*.

† Soraj Hongladarom is a Professor of Philosophy and Director of the Center for Science, Technology, and Society at Chulalongkorn University. He earned a PhD from Indiana University and lives in Bangkok, Thailand.

worthwhile other than simply describing ways of thinking of various people, then it would really be redundant.

In this paper I shall present a rather brief argument against this tendency. Specifically, I would like to show that philosophy is still viable and autonomous, and in order to do that I shall try to demonstrate how Thai philosophy is possible. That is, I would like to suggest a foundational path for Thai philosophy the same way Kant did in his laying a foundation for metaphysics. To answer questions of the type 'How is X possible?' is to demonstrate how X comes to be, what the limits are beyond which X is impossible. That is, to show how X is possible is to show its condition of possibility, to use the Kantian way of talking.[1] Hence, the condition of possibility of Thai philosophy, as will be shown in more detail below, is that Thai thinkers and philosophers begin to search for the optimal way of living, the best direction the community as a whole should take, while acknowledging that there can be no final answer to such questions. This is different from the usual sort of investigation in other disciplines in that there is no assumption of finality. Philosophy consists of a process, an unending one, but one necessary for the health of the community, as I will try to clarify in what follows.

The reason why it needs to be shown how Thai philosophy is possible is, firstly, that philosophical study in Thailand is still mostly limited to teaching the ideas and arguments of past or contemporary philosophers, both Western and Eastern. While this kind of study is very important, indeed indispensable, it is not a substitute for the kind of philosophical activity that should accompany it, which is an exercise in problem-solving ability where each party presents his or her own ideas regarding the issue in question and tries to convince the other through the use of reason and argument. The lack of such activity can be seen in there being only a handful of Thai philosophers who are active in proposing their own ideas to solve philosophical problems.[2] Another reason is related to the first, and might help to explain it. Thai culture is so imbued with Theravada Buddhist thought that Thai people in general do not see any need to look for solutions elsewhere, for it seems to them that Buddhism provides the solution to every possible philosophical problem; one only has to look back at the tradition to find them. Or if Buddhists have nothing to say about a particular problem, then they tend to conclude that the problem itself is not worth investigating, a waste of time.

However, the present situation in Thailand and elsewhere demands that this complacency in thinking be revamped. If Thai culture is to surge forward and remain responsive to the changes brought about by world conditions, then it has to become adaptive. This does not merely mean that Thai culture has to change and embrace elements from foreign cultures; Thai culture is already doing that. But what needs to change is the complacency in regarding Buddhism as providing the solution to every possible philosophical problem. To be complacent in thinking means one is stuck in one's own attitudes and ideas and cannot see beyond them. If one believes that Buddhism provides every answer, then one does not need to think for oneself. If one believes that the authority which justifies philosophical beliefs comes from Buddhism alone, then it seems that one will not be as responsive to the external circumstances as one should. For philosophy does not limit itself to the primary concerns of Buddhism, it is much broader and concerns itself with the complexities of the mundane world more than religion does. Thus, for some vexing philosophical problems which have a strong bearing on people's lives, such as the just distribution of limited resources, there does not seem to be a clear-cut answer. To depend wholly on Buddhism, believing that it can provide a real solution, then, would only mask the tendency to refrain from thinking and finding answers for oneself and for one's own society. The present circumstances of the world, characterised by their strong interconnections and dynamism, demand that members of each society be alert, active and responsive to change. Philosophy, in my conception at least, has a role in creating such a disposition.

## II. Two senses of 'cultural philosophy'

Before we take a close look at the demonstration, however, a rather important point needs to be clarified. In order to find out how Thai philosophy is possible, one has to be clear in what sense one uses

*Synkrētic*

the term 'Thai philosophy'. One is reminded of terms like 'Chinese philosophy', 'Indian philosophy', or 'Greek philosophy', which mean of course the philosophies of the respective traditions, each one having a long history. What these philosophies share is that they are an integral part of the cultural traditions in which each takes place. Thus, I chose to call them collectively 'cultural philosophy'. This is simply a term for referring collectively to all instances of 'Y philosophy', where 'Y' denotes a cultural or national entity. The philosophy constitutes what could be called the philosophical tradition, defined through shared canonical texts and sets of problems and methods. Examples are Plato's and Aristotle's writings in the case of Greek philosophy, Confucius' and Lao-Tze's in Chinese philosophy, and the Vedas in Indian philosophy. These texts partly define what it means to do philosophy in their respective traditions; they set out the problems and methods of philosophising. What is significant is that anyone can become members of these traditions, not by privilege of birth, but by subscribing to the same set of shared problems and methods constitutive of the respective traditions.

That is the first meaning of 'cultural philosophy'—a way of doing philosophy consisting of a shared set of texts, problems, and methods. However, there is another meaning which does not rely exclusively on the shared set of texts. According to this meaning, derived from Hegel's idea concerning the organicity of the social,[3] the culture or national identity of the philosophers is the criterion of cultural philosophy rather than the shared texts and methods. Thus, in this sense, a Chinese philosopher working on a problem in analytic philosophy, intended for a Chinese (possibly scholarly) audience, would be doing Chinese philosophy, for what matters now is neither the problems nor the shared methods, but the nationality or cultural identity of the philosopher who does the work. A Thai philosopher working on an interpretation of Confucius is not doing Chinese philosophy either. If he intends his work to be a service to the Thai people, and puts his own cultural identity into his interpretive work, then he is actually doing Thai philosophy.

So, a cultural philosophy can be construed in both ways. Indian philosophy thus becomes either the philosophy defined mostly by the Vedic tradition, or any kind of philosophical activity done by Indians for Indians. The second meaning might not seem at first glance to be a serious one. For what is so important about the nationalities of philosophers involved in a project? Perhaps this sense could be made clearer if one understood it to be an expression of a cultural or national entity in terms of philosophy. Thus, Thai philosophy in this sense is an expression, a manifestation, of the whole culture when it is engaging itself in philosophical activity. This does not sound as grandiose as it appears because the manifestation here is only what members of the cultural or national entity talk about, engaging themselves in a problem they find valuable and interesting. Here the focus is on the cultural entity, not the textual canon. Thus, to say that a cultural philosophy is such a manifestation is only to say that it is the activity of talking, discussing, arguing by members of the entity in question on a common topic. What makes the talk philosophical is that it is based on rational persuasion and the topics concern general matters about what is really valuable or whether the direction the society as a whole is taking is really a good one. This topic on the nature of philosophy will be discussed in the next section. The philosophical topic which members of a cultural or national entity talk about is here less important than the activity of talking and discussing itself. Hence, since such an activity generally occurs within the limit or terrain of a cultural or national entity, it then defines a philosophy of that culture.

Consequently, the example of the Thai engaging in interpreting Confucius can be seen as part of the concrete manifestation of the Thai culture in its reflexive activity of extending beyond itself in order to adapt itself so as to be responsive to changes. There is a caveat, though. The Thai who undertakes to interpret Confucius must do so in the context of Thai culture. That is, merely possessing Thai nationality or ethnicity is not a sufficient criterion to qualify as doing Thai philosophy. One has to "live within" the culture in question. This sense of living within is rather difficult to define, but one aspect of it is that one has to be a full member of the culture. For example, the Thai interpreting Confucius has to be Thai culturally. It will not do if the Thai grows up abroad and has little or no cultural ties with the homeland. In short, living within a culture includes the sense of belonging to that culture, a willingness to identify oneself as a member of that culture. Otherwise, the Thai here would really be doing Chinese philosophy had he grown up and imbibed aspects of Chinese culture so that he just became another Chinese. Another aspect of "living within" is that the philosophers' intended audience has to be made up of members of the culture he or she belongs to. This point is not difficult to grasp because if a Thai philosopher transmits his or her own philosophical viewpoints, not to members of his or her own cultural entity, but to those of another culture, then it could hardly be said that he or she is doing Thai philosophy.

Which sense is the correct one, then? Maybe the answer depends on our decision, and therefore the question is not an interesting one. What we really need, on the other hand, is a way to know how to achieve something valuable for us (read Thais) through the activities of talking, discussing, arguing. One has to realise that the authority of the self which serves as a basis for epistemological certainty is a thing of the past. At least that is my philosophical position, which of course cannot be argued for in full detail here.[4] Certainty does not lie within oneself, neither can it be found in an individual's relation to a reality outside. This does not mean that reality has no role, but that the relation to reality is always mediated by aspects of one's own cultural identity, webs of beliefs constituted not by an individual alone, but by the community of which he or she is a part. If this position is really a tenable one, then the activities of talking, discussing, etc. are crucial for gaining at least an insight into whether the direction in which the society or community as a whole is heading is the right one, or the most appropriate one considering the circumstances. These activities are what philosophers have always done. Not only philosophers, to be sure, but it seems that, owing to the nature of their discipline, philosophers are particularly apt for the job. And since these activities occur within the confines of a culture, or a community, then we can see the general picture of how such a cultural philosophy as the Thai one is to be possible.

## III. Philosophy as a reason-based activity in search of value

The two senses of cultural philosophy described above share a common trait in that they are both activities of talking, discussing, and arguing among interested parties. In the former sense, the interaction and arguments centre on the corpus of sacred texts or accepted practices and the interpretations and viewpoints offered are operative within this framework. In the second sense, the activities are more loosely based. They are not necessarily tied to a particular set of texts or practices. But since one cannot walk away from one's own cultural identity, the two senses of cultural philosophy are here conjoined at this juncture. On the one hand, merely sticking to the canonical texts and following canonical interpretations is hardly a way to remain responsive in the modern world; on the other hand, without such ties to the tradition, it appears that members of the cultural community are cut loose and have no-one to hold on to except themselves. If that were so, then there would really be no sense in which an activity could be termed Thai philosophy.

Hence, there is a sense in which both are correct; they are equally correct as instances of what philosophy is, or should be, in my conception. The aim of the discussions and arguments is ideally to arrive at consensus on whatever topic participating parties in the activities are interested in. But actually the ideal is not necessary, for it is the activity itself which is important. Philosophy in this conception is not a state where one is one with Reality, nor a movement toward that Reality, but a contested, conflicting condition where parties agree on some very basic condition needed for arguments to get going, such as the use and rules of logic, but disagree on almost everything else. Richard Rorty has argued that philosophy is actually a conversation among whoever is interested and has enough leisure to participate, with the purpose of just continuing the conversation.[5] However, if that is only the purpose there is for philosophy, then it is impossible to see how the conversation should be allowed to go on. If it is really the case that knowledge consists in individuals in a community depending on one another for challenge, revision, and support, then the activities of conversing and arguing become an important tool for the community to revitalise itself, to turn back upon itself so that it would not become redundant in a rapidly changing world. Philosophy in my conception consists of just such activity of arguing, discussing, talking, *etc.*, in other words activity whereby participants join in when they want to enter the debate, when they have something to say to the whole, when they either agree or disagree with any of the viewpoints offered to the members.[6] All occur under the umbrella notion that knowledge is to be found in such an activity. Since knowledge is a value term, in that to say of a proposition believed that it is a piece of knowledge is to commend it highly, then philosophy in this conception has a strong affinity with value.

I have argued elsewhere for this conception of philosophy as a rational activity consisting of debates, discussions, refutations, justifications, *etc.* on topics of a general nature which concern what the rest of the community finds valuable.[7] From the viewpoint of the community—a Hegelian perspective—the activities of the philosophers are manifestations of the community in its role as reflective thinkers and skeptical doubters. Philosophy for the community here is not a state whereby the community can claim that it has got in touch with Reality, whatever that may be. Philosophy explicitly attempts to dissociate itself from such finality. When there is finality, there is really no philosophy. Philosophy is a process, an activity.

Therefore, the possibility of Thai philosophy is straightforward. Thai philosophy is the activity of discussing, arguing, debating, refuting, affirming, *etc.*, all through the use of logical reasoning, to arrive at some kind of value which the community finds appealing. If such an activity happens in Thailand, *that* is Thai philosophy.

### IV. Thai philosophy as a reflective activity by and for Thais

As mentioned before, Thai Studies aims at understanding various aspects of Thai society and thus is an empirical investigation. Philosophy, being a normative discipline, therefore seems to have a tenuous relationship with it. However, a Thai conducting an investigation in Thai Studies is an instance of the Thai community reflecting on itself, and this is as it should be. And if the reflection eventually consists in rational debates (for it is hardly conceivable that when the community reflects on itself it would involve only one individual) on the question of values or some broad questions a methodology for which has not been settled, the activity of philosophising results. That is the way Thai philosophy is possible. Consequently, philosophy and Thai studies seem to be in much closer relationship than previously appeared. A normative and an empirical, descriptive discipline seems to be much intertwined.

Since we are Thai (after all I intend to address this paper to Thais), it is never possible that we stand back and try to look at our culture and way of life as if we were a foreigner. A distance afforded to the foreigner never materialises for us. This is the same for other people reflecting on their own culture as well. Note that this is not the same as saying that it is not possible for a foreigner to understand Thai society, or to have a detailed knowledge of it, for that would commit one to the fallacy of basing authority of knowledge on one's individual self, a philosophical theory which I am trying to dismiss. It is entirely possible that foreigners can have as thorough knowledge of Thai society as the best Thai scholars. However, since a Thai's perception of her own society is always clouded by her own cultural identity, while a foreigner's is not, what happens is that the foreigner can see something that Thais perhaps fail to see since it lies too close to take notice. Thus, sometimes we need to read what foreigners have to say about our own culture and society in order to put ourselves in their shoes and see things through their eyes. We gain fresh perspectives this way which may help us to break from the ties of culture and habit. Thai Studies by a Thai is, then, in principle different from what foreigners do to study our society. The former is an instance of self-reflection, while the other is not. Neither is superior nor inferior to the other; they are just different.[8]

An implication of this for Thai philosophy is that, since Thai studies by a Thai is an expression of the community's reflecting on itself, the discipline has a strong affinity to philosophy, despite the obvious differences. Thus, philosophy can indeed be a part of the collaborative, interdisciplinary effort of Thais to understand themselves, as well as that of members of the world community to understand Thais. What sets it apart is that philosophy is by nature reflective and skeptical, not, as usually understood, a mere set of doctrines to be described and catalogued. In this sense Thai philosophy, let me emphasise, is not just a set of doctrines, but the activities of Thai people when they enter into rational argumentation in order to understand deep questions that other disciplines find too intractable to study.

## V. Conclusion

So, Thai philosophy is possible through argument and discussion. Continuity with the past is also important, and plays a strongly formative role. It is what sets the activities occurring in Thailand apart from those of the same type occurring in other cultures. Whatever is distinctive of Thai culture is formative in the sense that it provides a scheme by which talks, debates, concerning deep values take place. However, since the activities themselves are by nature not limited within these horizons, the tradition thus affords only a starting point, a frame of reference which can be adapted or modified by the very members of that tradition themselves. This is just a fancy way of saying that the tradition is alive and responsive to outside developments. In this way, there is no need to be concerned that Thai philosophy in this conception is a break with the tradition or the past. It is merely the tradition itself, but in its active, dynamic role. Thai studies thus become in part an activity of Thais to understand themselves. There is no need to boast that this is the only way to understand Thai culture; in fact foreigners may have a better perspective than we do, since they are not hampered by biases or prejudices that shadow us. But without the Thai community reflecting upon itself, trying to see its role in the scheme of things as well as the overall meaning of what there is and what it means to be Thai, then such a community would remain locked within its self-imposed prison of tradition. Thai culture would thus become no better than a showpiece in a museum.

*How is Thai philosophy possible?*

## Notes

1 See Immanuel Kant, *Critique of Pure Reason* (New York: St. Martins, 1929), transl. Norman Kemp Smith. For example, A2/B6-A6/B10.

2 This can be seen from the sparse research done by members of philosophy departments throughout the country. Most of the research published in these few decades has been expository in nature, drawing mostly upon Buddhist sources. One reason for this may be the preferences of the individual researchers, but I think the more interesting and deeper reason is that Thai philosophers, being Thai and thus integral participants of the culture, feel that there is really no need to philosophise, as I have explained above.

3 See, for example, Charles Taylor's discussion of the Hegelian concept of *Sittlichkeit* in *Hegel* (Cambridge: Cambridge University Press, 1975), 376-378.

4 I have argued for this point extensively in *Horizons of Philosophy: Directions for Philosophy in Thailand* (in Thai), available at: <http://pioneer.chula.ac.th/~hsoraj/Horizon_of_Philosophy.pdf>.

5 Richard Rorty, *Philosophy and the Mirror of Nature* (Princeton: Princeton University Press, 1979), 377-379.

6 Thus, my conception differs from that of Jürgen Habermas, who in 'Philosophy as Stand-In and Interpreter' (in Kenneth Baynes, James Bohman, and Thomas McCarthy, eds. *After Philosophy: End or Transformation?* [Cambridge, MA: MIT Press, 1987], 296-315) argues for a conception of philosophy as one retaining a place for 'empirical theories with strong universalistic claims' (310). That is, philosophy will yield to such theories when they are capable of demonstrating their justified occupation. Thus, philosophy in this sense has a strong universalistic overtone. For Habermas it points to a way whereby universalist claims are possible. However, for philosophy to be able to hold such a place seems to presuppose that it could in some way point to the universal, even though philosophy does not in fact grasp it. But that is a very different conception of philosophy than the one presented here, which is derived from situations where visions of what constitutes the good life and so on collide, a conception that changes the aim of philosophy from establishing truth to seeing what good could come out of unfinalisable arguments.

7 Soraj Hongladarom, *Horizons of Philosophy*.

8 Thongchai Winichakul, in *Siam Mapped: A History of the Geo-body of a Nation* (Chiang Mai: Silkworms Books, 1994), 6-9, argues against claims made by traditional Thai scholars of Thai studies that Thai people know more about their subject matter than anybody else. I agree with him on this point. However, what seems to be missing from his account is that he does not provide a full reason in support of the thesis, nor does he see any merit in the conduct of Thai studies by Thais on the methodology based on what he calls 'the researchers' predetermined notion of what constitutes a Thai worldview' (8). I happen to disagree with him on both points. The first point seems to presuppose that Thongchai disapproves of a Thai studying her own society, but that is ironic, for Thongchai himself is a Thai, and thus necessarily subject to the same criticism he levels on the workings of other

Thais studying their own culture. Thongchai supposes that these Thai scholars uncritically think that they know what 'Thainess' means, and this forms a core of his criticism, having rejected the idea that 'Thainess' can have any fixed meaning (9). But 'Thainess' does not have to have fixed meanings in order for these Thai scholars to be able to do what they are doing, and doing well. The word could be defined extensionally, as logicians say. That is, there is no need to find a fixed meaning for the word, what is required is only that there be some tangible criteria to separate all Thai people from others, such as holding Thai passports, living within a certain geographical region, and so on. These requirements are not abstract and are actually in use to find out who is Thai and who is not. To press for any deeper meaning than this seems to me a case of philosophical illusion.

On the second point, Thongchai seems to be denigrating somewhat attempts by Thais to understand themselves. But what is wrong with having such a predetermined notion of Thainess? Apart from the notion of fixed meanings just mentioned, the works of these scholars can well be seen as manifestations of the Thai community to understand itself, and as such there is hardly any need to justify the meaning of 'Thainess' involved in the projects, for that is always assumed. Viewed from this perspective, Thongchai's own works, such as *Siam Mapped* but also other works which aim at understanding Thai society or its history, are likewise manifestations of this sort. Thongchai, to be sure, has a point in his criticisms, but one has to be aware that in a group's reflecting upon itself there is hardly any point in trying to separate oneself from the reflecting, as if it were possible to stand back outside the circle of one's own cultural identity and to find out which way of looking is the most truthful one.

# RESPONSES
*Kant and the Tahitians*

# A second birth in Tahiti

*Robert Koenig**

TRANSLATED BY *Daryl Morini*[†]

**Mr Koenig, you founded the publisher *Haere Pō* in 1981, which is well-known to all literary circles in the French-speaking Pacific. When did you arrive in Tahiti?**

I came to French Polynesia in September 1969 for my compulsory national service. I was a member of the civilian scheme called the *volontariat à l'aide technique*, a kind of Peace Corps at that time. Because I didn't want to do my military service, the French military and Protestant mission in Tahiti expedited my coming, even though I wanted to go to Africa. Which is why I'm still unable to critique either institution, grateful as I am to each of them. Teaching philosophy in the small Protestant college in Papeete was eye-opening, or rather a second birth among Polynesian families and communities. I was lucky enough to be born twice. Why should cats hold a monopoly on having nine lives?

---

[*] Robert Koenig is director of the Tahiti-based publisher *Editions Haere Pō*. He taught philosophy there, through which he discovered Tahiti and its islands with his wife Denise Koenig. They live outside Papeete, French Polynesia.

[†] Daryl Morini is a Canberra-based translator of Russian and French philosophy. He is editor of *Synkrētic*.

*A second birth in Tahiti*

**A unique path brings you to French Polynesia, that of philosophy.**

That's right. I taught philosophy or rather tried to teach it, and I remember throwing away all the lesson plans I had diligently prepared back in Alsace at the end of my second week in Tahiti. I took great pleasure in going to school for those 34 years, taking only two days off for my wedding and sick leave. I was fortunate enough to move around, teaching at Hermon Pastoral School, La Mennais Catholic College, and the Mamao School of Nursing—teaching my philosophy class each time. I delivered innovative lessons in civics on the political status of our islands and did my best to teach history and geography to junior college students in grades 6 and 5 [*ed.* – grades 7 and 8 in Australia] using the comic strip *Rahan* on prehistory and *Alix* on the Roman period.

***Haere Pō* books are beautiful and relevant to the whole Pacific region. When did this adventure begin?**

*Haere Pō* means "nightwalkers". This was chosen in response to Victor Segalen's *Immémoriaux*, the story of a *haere pō* who trips over one word.[1] This project was brought to life in 1981 by a group of friends, our passion for reading and learning, and the need to share what we felt by allowing people to read books we thought could help them to keep getting along. Our goal was to publish books that were entirely designed and printed in Tahiti, as in the early days of the London Missionary Society (LMS) across the Pacific, and in the official and unofficial languages of our islands. In French, Tahitian, Marquesan, in Paumotu, in "Australian", even in English. We were neither monocultural nor monolingual, but came from multiple backgrounds including Chinese, Tahitian, Alsatian, Swiss, even Swiss-German. This helps to understand and respect the complexity of insular places. We have now published around 110 books in 40 years.

**I understand that *Haere Pō* is an adventure which you have been on with your family.**

*Synkrētic*

Everything I say here—and everything I don't say—wouldn't have been possible without my wife Denise, who with loving care describes the sounds and colour of this world to me, colour-blind as I am!

**You have taught philosophy in Europe and the Pacific. How did these different cultural contexts modify your method of instruction?**

To try to teach philosophy in Tahiti means, firstly, doing everything you can to help students pass their written and oral exams to a respectable degree. That means writing dissertations on a given topic, providing coherent arguments over two or three sections while referencing classical sources, *i.e.* those taught in class. Philosophy has a delayed effect like some medications. With the only real question being whether curiosity, that is the desire to learn, can be taught. I would often try to inspire their desire for it using films, unusual documentaries, even books! I'd take them out to art exhibitions, to meet various prominent figures, and to observe court proceedings.

**Which Western thinker was most relevant in Tahiti? Was it Socrates?**

Some called my classroom "the cave". Plato or rather Socrates and his *Symposium* and the second of Nietzsche's *Untimely Meditations* were both at home in it. I preferred to ask questions, noting that *questio* is Latin for "to torture", rather than giving answers. Catechisms exist for those whose curiosity is limited.

**What differences have you observed between European and Polynesian philosophy?**

The myths from the edges of the Mediterranean gave birth to the philosophical tradition, but Oceanian shores saw myths flourish that were remarkably full of lessons on how to live, on life experiences either lived or imagined, and on the potential for breaking and tearing oneself away from life to live anew. Making students pay heed to this rich tradition by discovering it myself was unexpected.

## What did the Tahitian culture which you adopted teach you?

Living in Tahiti—around the time of the nuclear tests, of various tourism campaigns, and during its so-called cultural renewal and wokism—is to live in ancient, modern, and postmodern misconceptions and perhaps even prejudices. Meaning that it is to live in the ideas of those who live, think, dream in Königsberg, Berlin, Paris, London, Shanghai, and even Sydney. I often asked myself where and when I was living, hence my interest in and our books on the first contacts of European navigators and missionaries. While it's easy to write about what one saw or thought one saw, I always tried to make students read between the lines, which was the only way of preserving their adolescent eyes.

## In one of his works,[2] the philosopher Immanuel Kant criticises Tahitians and their accursed happiness. Was Kant sad, and did he envy their happiness?

I'm not sure if Kant was sad. Can a watch be sad? Kant was famous for the fact that one could set one's watch by observing him walking through Königsberg. If I recall correctly, he was "late" only once: after he read about the French Revolution in the newspapers. As for his attitude towards the Tahitians, is not thinking firstly thinking *against* something? Much as Kant did against Rousseau, against the simplifications of the myth of a "New Cytheria", meaning a romantic paradise, as the French navigator Louis-Antoine de Bougainville named Tahiti in 1768.

## If Kant had visited them, what would he have learned from the Tahitians?

It depends. In which period? Alongside Captain Cook and the Forsters on their second voyage from 1772 to 1775, when Kant was 48 years old? Or alongside LMS missionaries on the *Duff* in 1797? Perhaps he might have learned Tahitian like them using Peter Heywood's manuscript[3] at age 73! He could have gone to the Marquesas islands like William Crook[4] or returned to London on their ship. In any case, he could have been inspired to write his 1798 *Anthropology from a Pragmatic Point of View* completely differently.

**Is your publishing house confronted with the language barrier, which cuts off the English-speaking from the French-speaking Pacific like a great barrier reef?**

Regarding publishing, we tried to release books for the English-speaking public living outside French Polynesia. It was a total failure. *Too bad*, as you say in English. But the Great Ocean is something that can separate as much as it can unite. Isn't that what Epeli Hau'ofa, a great Tongan thinker and theologian, once said?[5] In the old days, the Spanish, British, French, German, and Japanese colonies drew borders across the so-called Great South Sea, and modern maps significantly extend these old borders with the addition of Exclusive Economic Zones. Could the Māori name for the Pacific, *Te Moana-nui-a-Kiwa* (which has nothing to do with the rugby team *Moana Pasifika*!), be a better alternative or a more holistic concept for half the surface of our Earth?

**So, are the Pacific's linguistic and cultural diversity more of an asset?**

Yes, I think so. Is not monoculture, whether agricultural or cultural, one of the factors behind a warming climate and nationalisms? Becoming aware of our biodiversity firstly means trying to be skeptical of what we see and hear, and not stopping there.

*A second birth in Tahiti*

# Notes

1. Victor Segalen (1878-1919) was a French naval doctor posted to French Polynesia from 1903-1905. This inspired him to write *Les Immémoriaux* about the religious conversion of Tahiti's Maohi people. See Victor Segalen, *A Lapse of Memory*, transl. Rosemary Arnoux (Brisbane: Boombana Publications, 1995).

2. 'Does the author really mean that if the happy inhabitants of Tahiti, never visited by more cultured nations, had been destined to live for thousands of centuries in their tranquil indolence, one could give a satisfying answer to the question why they exist at all, and whether it would not have been just as good to have this island populated with happy sheep and cattle as with human beings who are happy merely enjoying themselves?' Immanuel Kant, 'Review of J. G. Herder's *Ideas for the philosophy of the history of humanity. Parts 1 and 2* (1785)', transl. Allen W. Wood, in Robert B. Louden and Günter Zöller (eds.), *Anthropology, History, and Education* (Cambridge: Cambridge University Press, 2007), 142.

3. See Rolf E. du Rietz, 'Peter Heywood's Tahitian Vocabulary and the Narratives of James Morrison: Some Notes on their Origin and History', in *The Journal of the Polynesian Society*, Vol. 98, No. 1 (March 1989): 100-103.

4. William Pascoe Crook, *An Account of the Marquesas islands 1797-1799*, with an introduction by Greg Dening (Papeete: Haere Pō, 2007).

5. See, *inter alia*, Epeli Hau'ofa, *We Are the Ocean: Selected Works* (Honolulu: University of Hawaii Press, 2008).

# Kant's critique of idealised Tahitians

*Simon Swift\**

Professor Swift, in 2005 you wrote a fantastic paper on Immanuel Kant's critique of his former student J.G. Herder.[1] It's hard to think of an odder couple. I can't imagine Professor Kant enjoying marking Herder's papers.

Me neither! I guess something that's always really fascinated me and that filters through in my argument is the question of student-teacher relations. I'm especially interested in the question of how the work of the student often holds the teacher's thought in an intimate embrace while rejecting key aspects of it. Think Heidegger and Hannah Arendt, Paul de Man and Gayatri Spivak who also features in my article, and Kant and Herder. All of these were star students who later took umbrage at their teachers' doctrines.

When some people read Herder, Hamann, Nietzsche, or Shestov critiquing reason in what has been called the "counter-Enlightenment", it sets off alarm bells as if they were extremists. Is this a testament to Kant's legacy?

I think so, yes. It's testament to how normative Kant's view of reason became, and his sense that it needs to be protected against

---

\* Simon Swift is Associate Professor of Modern English Literature at Geneva University. Prof. Swift holds a PhD from Leeds and is the author of *Romanticism, Literature and Philosophy* (2008). He lives in Geneva, Switzerland.

'fanaticism'.² But I'd also want to temper that claim in two different ways.

First, while people like Nietzsche were very close, even if hostile readers of the morality of Kant's thinking, the rise of Kant-influenced ideas such as positivism and utilitarianism in the 19th century created a disconnect between Kant's legacy and what he really had in mind. This is especially the case when we think about what reason is and what it does. Kant's reason is a much more dynamic and lyrical force than the one of abstract calculation our inherited idea suggests.

**That's certainly the idea I have of Kant. But you see lyricism in his works?**

Yes, and part of that lyricism comes from Kant's efforts to save the Enlightenment by inoculating it with a dose of the kind of lyricism and 'enthusiasm'³ that he saw emerging in the work of people like Herder and Hamann. For Kant, this kind of thought didn't know what it was doing. By trying to shake up enlightenment, to make it sensitive to language, culture, and expression as forms of determination, it risked destroying enlightenment altogether.

I think that remains a real risk even now—so I guess I'm sympathetic to Kant's legacy! At the same time, he recognised that enlightenment needed to become responsive to ideas of history and embodiment—what we now take to be the counter-Enlightenment position.

But the second qualification would relate to what we mean by "counter-Enlightenment". How did those who opposed Kant's version of enlightenment in the 1780s impact later thinkers like Nietzsche, Marx, and Freud, who themselves shaped later critical theory, which sets out its own critique of enlightenment? I'm not sure that that's a question that we've adequately answered yet.

**Okay, so their dispute breaks out in 1785 because Professor Kant writes bad reviews—we're talking 1-star—of Herder's *Ideas on***

*Synkrētic*

*the Philosophy of the History of Mankind.*[4] **Fairly standard academic fare, but it seems personal.**

I think it definitely is. Kant was desperate to make a claim that reason is a public, communal act that depends upon its readers as 'co-workers', as he writes at one point. Kant wanted to be accessible, yet most people found his writing totally impenetrable. Herder, by contrast, was much easier to read, wilfully popular, and therefore something of a rising academic star in 1785.

But Kant thought that Herder's argument, and especially its use of poetical analogies, fooled readers into thinking they'd understood something about the cause of nature, which was still mysterious and impenetrable. For Kant, thinking is about collective hard work undertaken to try to advance in our understanding of a universe that is basically paradoxical and hard to explain. Kant, remember, didn't have the benefit of particle physics. So, for Kant, style plays an important role in calling others into that communal labour. But none of this sounds very sexy!

**So, it annoyed Kant that Herder successfully popularised philosophy?**

Because Herder seemed to give his readers easy access to complete answers in an enjoyable form, one can only suspect that Kant felt a bit betrayed that someone he'd taught had so wilfully abandoned the meticulousness of his thinking about nature and history. And undoubtedly, Kant was jealous of the success! It's not the first time that a philosopher or critic like Herder has got hold of some new ideas in science and spun a totalising metaphysics out of them—we still see that today. Kant would urge caution in making sense of science by those not trained in interpreting it.

**Kant rejects Herder's claim that our true goal in life is our own individual happiness, which is something like an article of faith of modern Western culture. So, is Kant saying that happiness isn't the point of our existence?**

He is. Here you begin to see why Herder seemed more sexy! Kant was a Protestant, after all, who thought that life was about labour and the life of the group rather than of the individual. So, one of the problems with establishing happiness as the purpose of life, for Kant, was that it seemed egotistical to him—as if my job is to establish my own satisfaction, rather than to build a better world for future generations by cooperating with those around me to achieve it. Here, I think we could understand Kant as a kind of forefather of eco-activism, which is all about imagining the consequences of our selfish actions in the future and building a better world for future generations.

At the same time, I think it's important to stress that Kant isn't saying that we should somehow aim to be miserable, or that happiness is bad. The fact that we find people who are happy in many different environments across the world suggests, in fact, that humans have a capacity to change their environments in ways that make them more satisfied—or so Kant would claim. And relatedly, he's also interested in ideas of rational happiness, the kind of contentment that we achieve by setting our own ends and realising them, as opposed to just going along with what we find around us.

**Here we get to Kant's famous quote that sparked its own share of academic quarrels. In attacking Herder's pæan to happiness, Kant asks why the Tahitians 'exist at all, and whether it would not have been just as good to have this island populated with happy sheep and cattle as with human beings who are happy merely enjoying themselves?'[5] What does this mean?**

It's hard to live with, isn't it? Kant is explicitly comparing non-European human life to the lives of animals, in order to suggest that both make problematic the idea that there is a purpose to human existence. And this as the colonisation of the Pacific is really getting under way. It's not in any way forgivable, but it's also important to look at what Kant says in context. We've seen that Kant is concerned with humans building a world for themselves, together, of their own rational design, and so he wrinkles his nose at cultures and environments that, from his European perspective, seem to be about satisfaction with what nature produces and show little desire to change it.

Yet Kant is actually more worried about Europeans who, reading stories about Tahitian life, might be drawn to it themselves. Herder's work is evidence, for Kant, of a growing hatred of rational life in the culture of the late Enlightenment, a desire to opt out of the civilisational process, which he found evidence of in the lure of Tahiti to the European imagination. Kant basically thought that this kind of opting out was selfish, but also insulting to the dignity of all humans, whether European or Tahitian.

**Fascinating. He was upset by Europeans opting out of his ideas, in a sense.**

So you could argue that he's more troubled by the surfer who wants to "get away from it all" on Tahiti than by the Tahitians themselves, because the surfer insists on Tahiti as a space that is outside of "it all", *i.e.* human cultural development, and that he wants to keep unspoiled for his own selfish purposes. Of course, Kant's ideas about the necessity of world-building look different to us, reflecting back on that moment through the intermediating history of genocide and ecocide. And it's undeniable that Kant imagines life outside of European civilisation as a life closer to the animals, and therefore a life less worth living.

**So, what Kant doesn't like is the claim that we can be happy apart from reason, that our happiness depends on feelings. It's interesting that Kant doesn't admire the cow's happiness. Nietzsche did.[6] Schopenhauer too.[7]**

For sure. One qualification I would make is that Kant doesn't necessarily think that reason and feeling are opposites. Recent critics have shown that Kant actually anticipates, in some ways, our more postmodern sense that reason is about embodiment.[8] He thinks that feeling and reason are deeply intertwined, and that we need to look at how each produces the other. But you are absolutely right that the capacity to forget and to not feel resentment, which Nietzsche associates with the cow, is not something you'll find in Kant. We are absolutely historical beings of time and memory, and imagining the future and how things might otherwise be is a bit of a waste of time for him.

**But why does a German professor who never left Königsberg take issue with the happiness of the Tahitian people *in particular*? Was he influenced by Bougainville, Diderot, or Captain Cook, whose visit to Tahiti he references?[9]**

Absolutely. I think he's interested in Tahiti because it's available to him in source texts, and also because it's attractive. But in passages equivalent to the one you cite above in other works Kant also talks about indigenous peoples from other places remote to Europe.

**There are many interpretations of Kant's metaphor. Is it racism as some argue,[10] a travelogue trope, a way for him to deflate Herder's noble savage myth by arguing that Tahitian happiness is impossible, or all of the above?**

First off, I think it absolutely is racism, no doubt. Kant is just a typical middle class European in assuming that life outside of what counts, for him, as civilisation, is closer to animal life. Remember too, though, that Kant is writing at the very moment of ethnography's birth. Later on, people like Claude Lévi-Strauss will come along to teach Europeans about how culture has many meanings beyond Europe's arrogant assumption to have a trademark on it. Yet I think it's also important not to stop there—wherever there is racism, it helps with the anti-racist struggle to try to understand where it comes from.

And Kant is one of those racists who is trying to be benevolent, as I've indicated above. There's a sense in which he's arguing that it's *Herder* who's the real racist by making of Tahiti a kind of refuge for the agitated European imagination. A bit like Edward Said has argued about European imaginings of Asia in *Orientalism*,[11] Herder's idealisation of a life untouched by reason could be racism in dis-

## Synkrētic

guise. For me, it seems incontrovertible that, on his own terms, Kant thinks that Herder's argument denies a true human vocation to Tahitians. In thinking this, he is clearly not much different than the missionary come to save souls. But I think that Kant's critique of Herder also tells us something more interesting about his argument that is easy to miss. Lots of critics have written about how Kant is, as it were, unconsciously drawing up a blueprint for colonial domination in phrases like the one you quote above. So, the idea would be that philosophy doesn't realise how up to its neck in geopolitics it is. It has a blind spot; its idea of itself is that it is just about ideas and it doesn't notice that it has a real effect in the world. I'd suggest, first, that that is unfair to Kant, and that he's always thinking about the importance of philosophy to the real world—he doesn't live in an ivory tower of abstraction.

But maybe even more interestingly, he *knows* he's being provocative in comparing Tahitians to animals. This is a riposte to Herder's idealisation of the noble savage idea which, if you read it through patiently, shows that idea to contain its own heavy dose of racism. At the very least, this calls into question the arrogance of the critic who thinks they know more about Kant's text than he does. None of which excuses the casual, unthinking racism though.

**At the end to your 2005 piece, you point to a literary quality to these symbols and analogies of Kant's, including that of the happy Tahitians.[12] That may be news to anyone who has attempted to read any of his three *Critiques*.**

No doubt! But actually, the *Critiques* don't necessarily deserve their forbidding reputation. I think it was the philosopher Jacques Derrida who said that the problem with the *Critique of Pure Reason* is that no one reads it backwards! If you just read the first half, all you have is really complex, taxing analytical and dialectical philosophy. And most people give up after 200 pages of that. But in the second part, especially Kant's 'Architectonic of Pure Reason', it becomes strange and beautiful, filled with amazing, hallucinatory metaphors of houses in wastelands, living statues, and so on. Again, Kant was desperate to make his work translate into the popular imagination but struggled to achieve that without compromising on the integrity of his ideas. But the efforts he makes to do so are much more interesting than people generally realise.

**Is it possible that no one is as happy as the tropes about smiling Tahitians, Nepalese, and ni-Van people suggest? And that, if the self-help books by happiness gurus that are sold by the million aren't helping, Kant was right?**

That would make for a sad world! There's a lot to be unhappy about today: war, the condition of refugees in our world, environmental collapse, economic inequality, racism, the psychological consequences of the pandemic. But I guess I remain a Kantian in my belief that we are at our happiest when we work together for the common good. And by "common" I mean truly common, involving not just every human being, but every sentient, living being on the planet.

Kant's text in some ways marks the moment when modern Western humanity entered on its suicidal course of colonisation, genocide, and environmental devastation—which is to say, when it finally had the tools it needed to maximise the devastation it had always practiced. But I also think that humans are stunning beings of consciousness, empathy, sociability and that Kant also modelled many of these ideas. We can serve each other as much as we harm each other. Let's hope that happiness can flourish through the former impulse winning out.

# *Synkrētic*

## Notes

1. Simon Swift, 'Kant, Herder, and the question of philosophical anthropology', in *Textual Practice*, Vol. 19, No. 2 (2005): 219-238.
2. Rachel Zuckert, 'Kant's Account of Practical Fanaticism', in *Kant's Moral Metaphysics*, eds. Benjamin James Bruxvoort Lipscomb and James K. Krueger (Berlin: De Gruyter, 2010), 291-318.
3. Religious 'enthusiasm' is a synonym for fanaticism. See Zuckert, 'Kant's Account of Practical Fanaticism', 291.
4. Also translated as J.G. Herder, *Outlines of a Philosophy of the History of Man*, transl. T. Churchill, Second Edition (London: J. Johnson, St. Paul's Church-Yard, 1803).
5. 'Does the author really mean that if the happy inhabitants of Tahiti, never visited by more cultured nations, had been destined to live for thousands of centuries in their tranquil indolence, one could give a satisfying answer to the question why they exist at all, and whether it would not have been just as good to have this island populated with happy sheep and cattle as with human beings who are happy merely enjoying themselves?' Immanuel Kant, 'Review of J. G. Herder's *Ideas for the philosophy of the history of humanity. Parts 1 and 2* (1785)', transl. Allen W. Wood, in Robert B. Louden and Günter Zöller (eds.), *Anthropology, History, and Education* (Cambridge: Cambridge University Press, 2007), 142.
6. Friedrich Nietzsche, 'On the Uses and Disadvantages of History for Life', in *Untimely Meditations*, ed. Daniel Breazeale, transl. R.J. Hollingdale (Cambridge: Cambridge University Press, 1997), 60.
7. Arthur Schopenhauer, 'On the Sufferings of the World', in *Studies in Pessimism*, transl. Thomas Bailey Saunders (London: George Allen & Unwin, Ltd., 1913): 9-30.
8. Christian Onof, 'Kant's conception of self as subject and its embodiment', *Kant Yearbook*, Vol. 2, Issue 1 (2010): 147-174.
9. Kant, 'Anthropology from a pragmatic point of view (1798)', transl. Robert B. Louden, in *Anthropology, History, and Education*, 401.
10. Jimmy Yab, *Kant and the Politics of Racism: Towards Kant's racialised form of cosmopolitan right* (Cham: Springer, 2021), 106.
11. Edward Said, *Orientalism* (New York: Vintage Books, 1978).
12. Swift, 'Kant, Herder, and the question of philosophical anthropology', 236.

# The whitewashing of Kant

*Robert Bernasconi*[*]

Professor Bernasconi, you wrote a 2005 paper called: 'Why do the happy inhabitants of Tahiti bother to exist at all?'[1] You were paraphrasing Kant, who you strikingly said 'unwittingly contributed' to a culture of genocide.

This is, as you point out, an old essay and I would certainly change some details if I were to rewrite it today. I had previously argued that Kant had in effect invented the modern scientific idea of race in terms of a permanent, that is to say hereditary, racial hierarchy. But this 2005 essay marks only an early stage in my attempt to address the role of a number of philosophers of history, and not just Kant, in promoting the idea that the very existence or purposefulness of some peoples was questionable because they could never attain the heights, the perfectibility, that was potentially open to the White race as a race. The actual phrase "bother to exist" was not my contribution; it is to be found in Robert Anchor's translation of Kant's review of Herder's *Ideen* published in Lewis White Beck's volume *Kant on History*. The translation of this phrase is not precise, but it captures perfectly the dismissive tone Kant frequently applied in his polemics.

---

[*] Robert Bernasconi is Edwin Erle Sparks Professor of Philosophy and African American Studies at Pennsylvania State University. He holds a DPhil from Sussex University and lives in Memphis, Tennessee, U.S.A.

*Synkrētic*

**You were not arguing that Kant had a direct, causal role in the events leading to later genocides, but that the famous Prussian had legitimised genocidal theories like many in his day. Is that a fair characterisation?**

Yes. Kant was certainly not advocating or celebrating the extermination of whole populations as later writers would do. But, as I pointed out in my essay, Kant himself recognised that if the meaning of the human species lay in its historical progress, there was an evident problem about the point of races and peoples that did not progress. For example, in lectures he delivered in 1778 he addressed the fact that Native Americans were in the process of dying out. He rejected as gruesome the idea of murdering them, but, given that he saw no role or need for them and indeed speculated that they would eventually kill each other as Europeans advanced into their land, he had articulated a dangerous perspective from which their presence could be seen as an obstacle to progress.

**It seems surreal that, as you say, Kant's thought on 'the question of the meaning of human existence' could possibly legitimise genocides. Many people couldn't imagine the quest for meaning being so dangerous. Is it?**

Kant's starting point in his 1784 essay on history was the apparent chaos of human affairs, which he contrasted with the orderliness visible in the way animals like bees and beavers go about their lives. Whereas nature's purposes for animal species was visible in each generation, it seemed to Kant that the meaning of human existence emerged only insofar as one took an historical perspective with regard to the species as a whole. But, having adopted this perspective, Kant was explicit that for nature's aim for humanity to be fulfilled earlier generations are in effect sacrificed for those that came later. And then the question becomes: What does that sacrifice look like?

**You explain that Kant was one of the first Western thinkers to detach this question of "meaning" from God and attribute it to**

history, from which he deduced his beliefs that Native Americans are a weak, talentless race, *etc.*

Or, more precisely, because he believed that their weakness and other limitations were hereditary, there was a problem about how they and races other than the White race contributed to the perfection of the species. It seemed that the logic of Kant's position about history when combined with his views about race entailed the idea that just as earlier generations sacrificed themselves for later generations, so the less talented races were called upon to sacrifice themselves for the White race that, as a race, was unique in possessing all the talents.

**You also write that Kant defended Native Americans against colonialism. Was this defence unusual for an 18th century European philosopher?**

Much is made of what he wrote about hospitality, but discussions of the right to hospitality were widespread throughout the eighteenth century. There was nothing significantly new there. By contrast, we must give him credit for insisting that the right to settle uninhabited lands did not include cases where there were shepherds or hunters. But there is an inner tension in his account. From his perspective using force to remove them was to the world's advantage, but at the same time he saw the injustice of doing so and he explicitly denied that civilising or Christianising supposedly savage inhabitants could override that. So, a Kantian would recognise the injustice of Indian Removal in the United States in the 1820s, while at the same time acknowledging that it was consistent with nature's aim.

**Kant, you write, held a teleological view of history on which our happiness as individuals was entirely dependent on some collective end state, such as cosmopolitanism, first being secured. This is still a popular way of thinking.**

## Synkrētic

Nobody today can look at the world and not see that the problems of world hunger, fighting disease, and combatting climate change can only be addressed by global cooperation. But those were not Kant's issues and that is not why he advocated cosmopolitanism. One should beware thinking that what Kant understood by cosmopolitanism is continuous with what the advocates of cosmopolitanism today (who nevertheless try to trade on Kant's name and attribute their own ideas to him) understand by that term. But buying into the Kant franchise is a much less attractive proposition now that his role in formulating what was effectively a new kind of racism is no longer concealed from the general public, as Kant scholars have frequently done since the Second World War, that is, until very recently.

**Which brings us to Kant's question of why the Tahitians 'exist at all, and whether it would not have been just as good to have this island populated with happy sheep and cattle as with human beings who are happy merely enjoying themselves?'[2]** What about their happiness so bothered Kant?

Kant was provoked by Georg Forster's description of Tahiti as one of the happiest spots on the globe, but his real target was Herder who understood that there was something inherently vicious about Kant's 1784 essay on history somewhat along the lines that I have already indicated. Herder believed that all peoples contributed to humanity. He celebrated their differences, but for Kant, although the white race possessed in principle all the talents, the other races were marked by limitations that were the product of the conditions in which they found themselves in the early stages of their existence. He viewed the happiness of the Tahitians as a product of the ease with which they were able to provide for themselves. But by living in such an environment they lacked the incentive to work and improve themselves and this had shaped their character. To Kant the source of their happiness was their downfall.

## The whitewashing of Kant

You write that philosophies of progress—in colonial, nationalistic, and pseudo-scientific forms—became bound up with mass murder in the 20th century. Has this potential link you posit been broken in our day and age?

I believe that there were significant changes, one might say paradigm shifts, that separate the racisms of the late eighteenth century from those of the early twentieth century, so I was not charting a continuous line of development. But I would add that some of the ways that Kant thought about race—his insistence on its hereditary character, his antipathy on biological grounds toward race mixing, and perhaps above all his importation of those two ideas into a progressive philosophy of history—were at very least unusual in his own time and anticipate in some respects what came later. To that extent one can say, with appropriate reservations, that they prepare the way for the biopolitics that took hold in the late nineteenth century. The idea of progress, like that of civilisation, is still frequently associated with some peoples and some races and not other peoples and races, even though we seem to have every reason to question the ideas of progress and civilisation themselves. Unfortunately, the culture of genocide, cultural and physical, is alive and well and the echoes of earlier philosophies, including Kant's, can be heard in it.

More recently, you wrote on the so-called second thoughts question, *i.e.* the debated claim that Kant substantially rethought his views on race in later works.[3] Have the views you have set out above been altered by this debate?

The idea that Kant changed his mind late in the day has proved very attractive to a number of scholars, even though what evidence there is for such a change is slight and is in any case confined to relatively minor points, given the larger picture. But there have recently been some strong responses critical of the second thoughts thesis. They not only largely vindicate my position, but even demonstrate that things are worse for Kant's reputation than I had imagined ten years ago. I have learned a lot from these new studies.

*Synkrētic*

**If Kant was wrong in making happiness subservient to ideas like progress, how do we learn from his failure as we try to live morally in our own time?**

I would be surprised if many people today still want to promote a philosophy constructed around either happiness or progress. Neither of these ideas speak to the moral and political issues of our time. But when it comes to living morally today, one prerequisite is intellectual honesty. There is a fundamental dishonesty in the attacks on critical race theory by politicians in the United States and it is mirrored in the way that academic philosophers have sought to whitewash the role of a number of canonical philosophers, not just Kant, when they promoted slavery and a racially based philosophy of history. In my view, we should be focusing more on the current crises and much less on trying to rehabilitate past philosophies. To that extent, I regret the fact that I have had to spend so much of my time having to show the deficiencies of past philosophies that still have adherents who want to defend them. But I judged it necessary to do so in order to create the space where other approaches might flourish and I believe we are seeing signs that there is now a strong appetite for radical change in the way philosophy is taught.

## Notes

1. Robert Bernasconi, 'Why Do the Happy Inhabitants of Tahiti Bother to Exist at All?', in *Genocide and Human Rights: A Philosophical Guide*, ed. John K. Roth (New York: Palgrave Macmillan, 2005), 139-148.

2. 'Does the author really mean that if the happy inhabitants of Tahiti, never visited by more cultured nations, had been destined to live for thousands of centuries in their tranquil indolence, one could give a satisfying answer to the question why they exist at all, and whether it would not have been just as good to have this island populated with happy sheep and cattle as with human beings who are happy merely enjoying themselves?' Immanuel Kant, 'Review of J. G. Herder's *Ideas for the philosophy of the history of humanity. Parts 1 and 2* (1785)', transl. Allen W. Wood, in Robert B. Louden and Günter Zöller (eds.), *Anthropology, History, and Education* (Cambridge: Cambridge University Press, 2007), 142.

3. Robert Bernasconi, 'Kant's Third Thoughts on Race', in Reading Kant's Geography, eds. Stuart Elden and Eduardo Mendieta (Albany: SUNY Press, 2011), 291-318.

# Tahiti in the European mind

*Chunjie Zhang**

Dr. Zhang, you are an expert on the role of the Pacific in 18th century German culture, an often forgotten colonial power. In the Pacific, Britain and France are usually seen as the leading colonisers.

Yes, when we think about colonialism and imperialism, the common association is the British Empire along with French or Dutch colonial enterprises in the twentieth century. The colonialism of the second German Empire was short-lived around 1900 and upended with WWI. Germany did not experience a wave of decolonialisation movements after WWII, like Britain or France. The lack of a lengthy colonial history in the German empire does not necessarily mean a lack of intellectual and cultural discourse of colonialism in Germany. My work on German-speaking culture and the Pacific aims to shed more light on the active role that German intellectuals played during the long eighteenth century while major colonial powers in Europe were exploring possibilities to establish colonies worldwide. The German intellectual and literary discourse substantially influenced Europe-wide discussions on racism, slavery, abolition, and colonial trade and exploitation.

---

\* Chunjie Zhang is Associate Professor of German at the University of California, Davis and works on 18th century European literature and philosophy. She holds a PhD from Duke University and lives in Davis, California, U.S.A.

*Synkrētic*

In your book *Transculturality and German Discourse in the Age of European Colonialism*,[1] which built on your doctoral work,[2] you write about Georg Forster who went to Tahiti with Captain Cook in 1772-1775.[3] He was torn between the ideas that it was a paradise and uncivilised. Was this ambivalence towards Tahiti common?

Forster provided a unique perspective due to his special status as a scientist onboard Cook's expedition and his foreigner status of being ethnically German with a work contract for the British. His travel writing, translated from English into German by himself, was a huge success in Germany and established the South Sea myth of paradise in central Europe. I think Forster was more impressed and fascinated with Tahiti rather than dismissing it as "primitive". He was torn between his admiration for Tahiti and his choice of not staying there for good. My point is that Forster was strongly influenced by the Tahitian way of life and he transported this admiration back home to Germany. It is the sustained impact of Tahiti on the European mind that has not been emphasised enough.

**You note that Forster's travel writings—and his 1778 book *Voyage Round the World*[4] in particular—shaped European ideas about Tahiti, which for context you note was then the second most popular genre after novels.**

Yes, travel writings were very popular, even though the novel was still an emerging genre that aroused a passion for reading (among young women) and, at the same time, skepticism and critique of this fervent interest. It may be a bit similar to today's videogames. But travel writings were an important repository of ethnographic knowledge and cultural-philosophical speculations about non-European places in European tradition. Forster managed to turn travel writing into a serious science.

**Very interesting. It's easy to forget the role of the Pacific in European culture. You compare the impact of Forster's work then**

to 'the landing on the moon and having an astronaut at one's dinner table in the 1960s.'

Haha, yes, Forster was invited to German courts and instantly became a celebrity after the German publication of his *Voyage Round the World*. He was offered a position as a natural history professor at the Collegium Carolinum in Kassel. That solved his financial issues, which had been caused by his father's feud with the British Admiralty over his right to publish his own travel writings.

**The naturalist Alexander von Humboldt, who visited Australia among other places, also saw his mentor Forster as a world authority on Tahiti and other 'happy islands of the Pacific'. Was that happiness trope popular back then?**

Yes, Humboldt grew up steeped in this South Sea myth and sees Forster as an authority on the matter of scientific travel writing. Indeed, Forster endeavoured to write a fact-based travelogue instead of a fantasy-filled account to quench consumers' thirst for curiosity. That ideal served as a model for Humboldt.

**Were Rousseau's theories a direct influence on Forster's idea that Tahiti was an earthly paradise, or is it more the case that both men drank from the same cultural waters?**

Rousseau's theory of the noble savage was indeed very influential in the eighteenth century. Yet, from my reading of Forster's writing, I feel that Forster was more directly influenced by what he experienced in Tahiti rather than imposing preconceived ideas on the Tahitians. Of course, Forster was not completely prejudice-free, but he strived to write based on his scientific findings instead of looking at things as though through 'coloured glass', as he terms it.[5] That's why I consider Forster's writing remarkable in the eighteenth century.

**Another part of this Edenic myth equated Tahiti with sexual freedom, as captured by the traveller Bougainville's and philosopher**

Diderot's writings, and in Paul Gauguin's paintings later. Even king Frederick William II had a strange Tahitian fantasy. This was totally mainstream in Europe, wasn't it?

That's correct. The idea of paradise is deeply connected to the satisfaction of our basic desires. Freud's psychoanalysis could be largely seen as a critique of the social suppression of desire in the Victorian era. The European sailors' experiences in Tahiti and the South Sea in general fuelled the fantasy of unrestrained sexuality, quite unlike the Christian mores in Europe. At the same time, a thinker like Denis Diderot used this hearsay to enunciate his critique of the Catholic Church during the Enlightenment. Gauguin used East Asian Buddhist paintings to portray nudity in a Tahiti of his fantasy. Thus, Forster's contribution to a more or less factual account of Tahiti was even more valuable vis-à-vis the other ends Tahiti was made to serve in the European imagination.

In a review of his former student J.G. Herder, even philosopher Immanuel Kant famously asked why Tahitians bother to 'exist at all', and whether it would not have been better for 'happy sheep and cattle' to live there if being happy is all the Tahitians do.[6] Why did he so disdain Tahitian happiness?

I am not quite familiar with this expression of Kant's. If it is true, it is definitely an arrogant and ignorant European colonial attitude to dismiss other cultures. At the same time, Kant was very interested in non-European cultures. He was an avid reader of travel writings, befriended seamen at the port city of Königsberg, and lectured regularly for decades on the anthropology, geography, and botany of the world in his lecture course on physical geography. Indeed, Kant developed his theory of race in his book *Anthropology* as part of the lecture script of this course.

Kant never went to Tahiti—he never left Königsberg. So, did his views rest on the same European clichés about Tahiti which he inherited uncritically? Or did they reflect his own racism as some argue,[7] or some other factors?

Kant was an avid reader of travel writings and enjoyed conversing with seamen about their experience abroad. Kant, as well as many other European thinkers of the time, was keenly interested in systematising the "findings" of the European expeditions into categories and typologies. Kant's racism was a product of his time, along with the dismissive language about Africans and Asians. Yet this happened before the dominance of European imperialism between 1850 and 1950. However, the coloniser's use of such philosophical accounts as authority to justify and support colonial exploitation and racial discrimination in policies and laws is a different issue.

**You worked on German cultural ties with China, Japan, India, Vietnam, and the Pacific. That's fascinating. Is there much interest in Germany today in the cultures of former Pacific colonies, parts of PNG and Solomon Islands?**

Franz Kafka's short story *In the Penal Colony* (1919) is set in the Pacific, I believe. The contemporary Swiss-German writer Christian Kracht's novel *Imperium* (2012) is set in German New Guinea. There is also a wave of decolonisation in German and European museums these days to return looted artefacts, mostly to African countries. But I am not sure whether the Pacific Islands were among the countries that would receive any repatriations.

## Notes

1  Chunjie Zhang, *Transculturality and German Discourse in the Age of European Colonialism* (Evanston, IL: Northwestern University Press, 2017).

2  Chunjie Zhang, 'Views from the Other Side: Colonial Culture and Anti-Colonial Sentiment in Germany around 1800', Doctor of Philosophy, Department of Germanic Languages and Literature, Duke University, 2010.

3  Johann George Adam Forster (1754-1794), known also as Georg Forster, was a German naturalist who at the age of 17 took part, then as an assistant to his father Johann Reinhold Forster (1729-1798), in James Cook's second expedition to the Pacific. He was a major figure of the Enlightenment in Germany and maintained a

correspondence with Georg Christoph Lichtenberg, some of whose work features in this issue of *Synkrētic*.

4   George Forster, *A Voyage Round the World in His Britannic Majesty's Sloop, Resolution, commanded by Capt. James Cook, during the Years 1772, 3, 4, and 5* (London: B. White et al., 1777). This work is in the public domain and available on archive.org.

5   Carina Pape, '"Race", "sex", and "gender": Intersections, naturalistic fallacies, and the Age of Reason', in *Modernity and its Ramifications*, ed. Martin L. Davies (London: Routledge, 2016), 160.

6   'Does the author really mean that if the happy inhabitants of Tahiti, never visited by more cultured nations, had been destined to live for thousands of centuries in their tranquil indolence, one could give a satisfying answer to the question why they exist at all, and whether it would not have been just as good to have this island populated with happy sheep and cattle as with human beings who are happy merely enjoying themselves?' Immanuel Kant, 'Review of J. G. Herder's *Ideas for the philosophy of the history of humanity. Parts 1 and 2* (1785)', transl. Allen W. Wood, in Robert B. Louden and Günter Zöller (eds.), *Anthropology, History, and Education* (Cambridge: Cambridge University Press, 2007), 142.

7   Robert Bernasconi, 'Will the real Kant please stand up: The challenge of Enlightenment racism to the study of the history of philosophy', in *Radical Philosophy*, Issue 117 (January/February 2003): 13-22.

# The colour blindness of reason

## *Eunah Lee**

Assistant Professor Lee, you wrote a 2018 book chapter[1] in which you argue, in the debate on Kant's racism, that he never really recanted it and that it is woven into his thought. Before getting to this, when did you first read Kant?

My first experience of reading Kant was as an undergraduate student at Seoul National University. I read parts of his works including his three *Critiques* in my various coursework, but his essay 'What is enlightenment?', which I read in a social philosophy course, left me with the most vivid impressions. Then I had opportunities to study Kant with Dr Jeff Edwards at Stony Brook University in the U.S. and later with Dr Andrea Esser at Marburg University in Germany during my doctoral program. I always had, and still have, a love-hate relationship with Kant.

**Some readers who associate Kant with his moral philosophy may be surprised by this racism debate. When did it start?**

Kant is best known for his ethical concepts like the categorical imperative, according to which we should do what could be willed to become universal moral laws and never treat other persons

---

\* Eunah Lee is Assistant Professor of Philosophy at St. Joseph's University. She earned her BA and MA at Seoul National University and PhD in philosophy at Stony Brook University. She lives in Long Island, New York, U.S.A.

merely as a means but as ends in themselves. But even in earlier research Kant's thoughts on different races were not a secret. I believe his racist ideas started to receive more public attention and critical illumination through anti-racist social and intellectual movements in our time, such as critical race theory. Although the historian E.H. Carr said this of history in general, the history of philosophy seems to be an unending dialogue between the present and the past.

**This interest in Kant's anthropology and concept of race may be striking in and of itself. I wasn't taught Kant in this light. The focus in my political science lectures was on his cosmopolitanism and perpetual peace theory.**

I, too, was introduced to Kant's philosophy through his universal moral law in my ethics course and to his cosmopolitan ideas in my political philosophy course. Ironically, I became increasingly interested in his racist remarks while working on my doctoral dissertation on Kantian and Hegelian cosmopolitanism. As I delved deeper into his philosophy of history, I was introduced to his anthropological works, where I encountered these striking and troubling remarks on non-white races. As a non-white woman, I wrestled with these passages and wrote the last chapter of my dissertation on the problem of race in Kant.

**You write that 'Kant *develops* his theory of race, which is a sign that it is not a regrettable personal prejudice, but the product of extended philosophical reflection.' Is a consensus forming in that direction, or is this still debated?**

I encounter increasingly more critical voices rather than those seriously defending Kant in this regard. Should we take this as a sign of a consensus among scholars? I am not sure. My observation could be due to the AI's algorithmic suggestions based on my intellectual predilection or political orientation. I believe the debate is still going on. The critical spirit and the willingness to defer seem to be the *modus operandi* of philosophers.

Some have argued that Kant was, to some extent, ahead of his time in defending the rights of Native Americans and other non-white groups, even as he described them as weak and lazy. What is Kant's record on this point?

In his *Toward Perpetual Peace* (1795), Kant proposes the establishment of a league of nations in which different peoples would live peacefully side by side. This is where Kant mentions the somewhat virtuous characters of other races. For one, he acknowledges the military courage of Native Americans being akin to that of the mediæval European knights. Some scholars emphasised these records as an indication that he recanted his 'earlier' racist views as they differ from his downright hostile assessments of non-white races in other writings. My article refuted this view for being too charitable. Kant's notion of cosmopolitan right does not require a strong egalitarian view of the different races, as many defenders would wish it did.

One anecdote you cite as among the egregious cases of Kant's racism is his review of J.G. Herder's work in which he asks why Tahitians bother to 'exist at all' if they're just as happy as cattle.[2] What is going on in this quote?

Johann Gottfried von Herder (1744-1803) was a contemporary of Immanuel Kant, and in fact Kant's former student. Both Kant and Herder wrote about the 'universal history of humanity,' a genre popular among 18th and 19th century Enlightenment thinkers. Kant's 'Idea for a universal history with a cosmopolitan aim' (1784) and Herder's 'Ideas for the philosophy of the history of humanity' (1784) were good examples of this genre. These works attempt to discover humanity's meaning and purpose by examining the course of history. This teleological historiography enabled them to explain past events from the perspective of progress and predict future paths. Kant was invited to review Herder's work, which he did in 1785.

*Synkrētic*

One notable difference between Kant and Herder was that Herder seemed more reluctant to use the notions of different human races than Kant. Herder envisioned borderless humanitarianism in contrast to Kant's version of a loose community composed of different nations. Perhaps this difference in their vision could explain their different attitudes toward other races. Also, Herder opposed Kant's idea that humanity will fully reach its perfection *as a species*, not as individual human beings. This is noteworthy because Kant maintained that humanity could reach its highest stage by the European white, denying other non-white races this privilege.

The infamous passage 'why do they [the happy inhabitants of Tahiti] exist at all?' comes from this context. Kant's rhetorical question assumes the Tahitians are awakened from their idleness by the visitors from more civilised nations, through whom they could achieve a higher stage and also play a role in the overall history of humanity. This passage is often viewed as his justification for colonial expeditions and enslavement, although Kant criticised the harsh treatments of enslaved people elsewhere.

**Is there anything in Kant's philosophy of history or anthropology that predisposed him particularly badly towards the Tahitians, or that placed them on a lower rung of an imagined ladder of civilisation in his eyes?**

Many European authors of the 18th century depended on travellers and explorers such as James Cook (1728-1779) or Sydney Parkinson (1745-1771) in their understanding of peoples living in distant places. Herder, who quotes extensively from ethnographic descriptions of these travelogues, also expressed a wish for a collection of portrayals and more faithful paintings of different people. So, whether in Kant's negative judgment toward 'backward people' or in Rousseau's notion of 'noble savage' in the other direction, the philosophers had to work with limited information as a window to vastly diverse ways of life.

If I have to point out something that might have predisposed Kant badly toward the Tahitians, I think it originates in his fundamental anti-hedonism. For Kant, the goal of human life is not to idle in a happy state but to strive for perfection through labour, to be worthy of happiness. From this point of view, Tahitians living in their 'tranquil indolence' are comparable to 'sheep and cattle' peacefully grazing in nature's abundance as they have not achieved, nor were actively working toward, a civilised state.

**The claim that Kant's comments on race do not invalidate his philosophy, you argue, is evidence of 'colour-blindness' in philosophy. With interest in race apparently growing worldwide, do you still see this as the case today?**

I did not intend to go so far as to claim that his racism invalidates his philosophy in its entirety. That would be too radical a claim for me. Although I am sympathetic to such a view, my claim is much more modest. I contend we must present and teach these edifying thinkers in all their complexities and tensions without idolising them by concealing their weaknesses or offering apologies. As a comparison, one may denounce Martin Heidegger's metaphysics for the reason that he was a Nazi member at one point. Although true, I do not want his Nazism to serve as an excuse not to study Heidegger. Instead, it behoves us to work harder to understand where and how his thinking allowed him to agree with and work for such a totalitarian regime.

When I think of Kant's racist remarks, I am reminded of what he said about his concept of 'inner freedom' or freedom of thought, which he defined as 'the freedom from the chains of concepts and ways of thinking that are habitual and confirmed by general opinion; - a freedom that is *not at all* common, so that even those who confess loyalty only to philosophy have only rarely been able to work themselves all the way up to it.'[3] I am afraid that Kant, a marvellous and magisterial thinker though he is, was not entirely freed from the chains of habitual concepts and general ways of thinking despite his own warnings and precaution.

*Synkrētic*

**If scholars come to agree that Kant's works were in fact irremediably racist, what do you think that will mean for how, or whether, his works are taught?**

It would be hard to predict if scholars could ever agree if Kant was an irremediable racist and, even if he were, how deeply his racism affected various branches of his philosophy. However, the ways in which Kant's works are taught need significant changes. In introducing his proposal for everlasting peace, we also need active discussions on his troubling ideas. One way to bring about such change is to expand canons so that students can be exposed to diverse authors from marginalised and oppressed groups. And this requires conscious efforts to excavate these groups' writings and uncover their thoughts.

For example, juxtaposing Quobna Ottobah Cugoano (c. 1757-c. 1791) with Kant could be an illuminating way to situate Kant's own prejudices. Cugoano, also known as John Stuart, was a native of the West African British colony of the Gold Coast. He was enslaved and shipped to the West Indies, and later worked as an abolitionist after being freed in Britain. His *Thoughts and Sentiments on the Evil of Slavery*,[4] published around the same time as Kant's anthropological works, serves as proof of the talent of non-white races, which Kant denied.[5] Cugoano powerfully argues that 'the Africans, though not so learned, are just as wise as the Europeans; and when the matter is left to human wisdom, they are both to err.' Criticising those who justified slavery based on revelation or reason, he writes that such pretences and excuses to deem any particular set of men inferior are 'the grossest perversion of reason, as well as an inconsistent and diabolical use of the sacred writings.'

**Which parts of Kant's project do you think will outlive his prejudices?**

I jokingly recall that one of my college professors would not encourage students to dwell on Kant's anthropological pieces because they are not Kant's 'essential' works. But who gets to decide what is essential and inessential to us? Kant's ethical concepts provide us with formidable antitheses to the sweeping consequentialist ideas in Western philosophy. Because of this significant contribution and the symbolic place Kant has, I believe readers or scholars have often neglected or downplayed his racist remarks.

## Notes

1 Eunah Lee, 'Race and the Self-Defeating Character of Kant's Argument in *Anthropology from a Pragmatic Point of View*', in *Natur und Freiheit: Akten des XII. Internationalen Kant-Kongresses*, eds. Violetta L. Waibel, Margit Ruffing, and David Wagner (Berlin: De Gruyter, 2018), 2737-2744.

2 'Does the author really mean that if the happy inhabitants of Tahiti, never visited by more cultured nations, had been destined to live for thousands of centuries in their tranquil indolence, one could give a satisfying answer to the question why they exist at all, and whether it would not have been just as good to have this island populated with happy sheep and cattle as with human beings who are happy merely enjoying themselves?' Immanuel Kant, 'Review of J. G. Herder's *Ideas for the philosophy of the history of humanity. Parts 1 and 2* (1785)', transl. Allen W. Wood, in Robert B. Louden and Günter Zöller (eds.), *Anthropology, History, and Education* (Cambridge: Cambridge University Press, 2007), 142, AA 8:65.

3 Immanuel Kant, 'Review of J. G. Herder's *Ideas for the philosophy of the history of humanity. Parts 1 and 2* (1785)', transl. Allen W. Wood, in Robert B. Louden and Günter Zöller (eds.), *Anthropology, History, and Education* (Cambridge: Cambridge University Press, 2007), 135, AA 8:57.

4 See Quobna Ottobah Cugoano, *Thoughts and Sentiments on the Evil of Slavery* (Penguin: London, 1999). The original title reads *Thoughts and Sentiments on the Evil and Wicked Traffic of the Slavery and Commerce of the Human Species* (1787).

5 Immanuel Kant, 'Physical Geography', in *Natural Science*, ed. Eric Watkins (Cambridge: Cambridge University Press, 2012), AA 9:316.

# Kant's impure ethics

*Robert Louden**

Professor Louden, you are one of the editors of a major 2007 collection of Kant's works called *Anthropology, History, and Education*.[1] The book has been cited 530 times and its chapters over 1,000 times each. How did this project start?

*Anthropology, History, and Education* (*AHE*) is a volume in *The Cambridge Edition of the Works of Immanuel Kant in Translation*. I was initially invited to translate Kant's works on education for this volume, and my role later expanded to that of co-editor (with Günter Zöller) and translator of *Anthropology from a Pragmatic Point of View*. I am also co-editor and translator of a second, related volume in this series.[2]

I'd like to return to one piece in this volume in a moment. But first, about your interest in Kant more generally, do you recall which of his works you first picked up and what effect they had on your thought?

I have always been primarily interested in Kant's *practical* philosophy—particularly his ethical theory. But like many readers of Kant, I initially found the abstractness of his ethical theory intimidating, and this is part of what led me to his more empirical writings

---

\* Robert Louden is Distinguished Professor of Philosophy at the University of Southern Maine. He earned a PhD in philosophy at the University of Chicago and lives in Portland, Maine and Honolulu, Hawaii, U.S.A.

and lectures on ethics and human nature. However, I do believe that anyone with serious interests in Kant should examine his entire corpus. For me, the question of how the different parts of his system do (or don't!) fit together has always been a very challenging puzzle.

**In 2000, you wrote a book with the intriguing title of *Kant's Impure Ethics*.[3] Does this impurity refer to the content of his ethics, e.g. people are morally impure, or to something else?**

In *Kant's Impure Ethics* I was intentionally playing with an ambiguity in the word 'impure'. For Kant, 'impure' means empirical or *a posteriori*, and my main argument was that his ethics contains more empirical or *a posteriori* content than most readers realise. But in ordinary speech, 'impure' means unclean or dirty, and I was also implying that his ethics is impure in this second sense as well.

**In this book, you touch on the hotly debated question of Kant's comments on Indigenous and non-white populations. Did your 2007 book, which translates relevant passages, start the debate on Kant's attitude to race?**

'Start' is an overstatement. Extracts of Kant's writings on race were published back in 1963 in a book edited by Gabriele Rabel,[4] and several of Mark Mikkelsen's more recent translations[5] were also published a few years before the ones in *AHE*. But I suspect that *AHE* has played a role in the English-language debate on Kant's attitudes toward race.

**In one piece, while writing an unfavourable review of a book by J.G. Herder, Kant criticises Tahitians for being as happy as cattle. He asks why they 'exist at all' if that's all they do.[6] Why did their enjoyment bother him?**

Unlike many contemporary ethical theorists, Kant holds that we have duties *to ourselves* as well as to others. Indeed, on his view, duties to ourselves are the foundation and pre-condition of all duties. The duty to develop one's talents is one of the primary duties to

## Synkrētic

oneself, but it is also an *imperfect* duty (it doesn't prescribe exactly what to do, but merely presents us with a broad goal to pursue). Individual agents need to use their discretion in deciding how best to fulfil this duty, after carefully assessing their own particular situation and interests. Some agents will choose to develop their athletic talents, others will strive to become musicians, *etc*. But to choose not to develop *any* of one's talents, which is how Kant reads the Tahitians, is a basic violation of one's duty, in addition to being inconsistent with the categorical imperative.

**You have argued that this quote is often misunderstood, that Kant wasn't attacking the Tahitians *per se* but was critiquing human beings everywhere who are just enjoying themselves.[7] But, still, why is that a problem for Kant?**

Kant reads people who are 'just enjoying themselves' as people who have intentionally decided not to cultivate *any* of their talents and rational capacities—again, a violation of duty that is inconsistent with the categorical imperative. Part of what he means here is that such a decision cannot be universalised without contradiction. If everyone were to make such a decision, humanity would not survive.

**Some argue that Kant's comments on the Tahitians are proof of his racism[8] and of the genocidal seed in his ideas.[9] You have written that Kant did not defend the genocide of non-Europeans.[10] Was he racist towards Tahitians?**

Yes, clearly Kant was 'racist towards Tahitians'—as well as towards all other non-whites. But when he writes that the non-white races will eventually die out, he is making an empirical prediction (one that was unfortunately shared by a great many white colonialists in the nineteenth and early twentieth centuries). He is not advocating the mass murder of specific racial groups. As he remarks in the *Pillau* anthropology lecture:

We find peoples who do not appear to have progressed in the perfection of human nature, but have reached a standstill, while others, such as the Europeans, are always progressing…[I]t appears that all of the Americans will be wiped out, not through acts of murder—that would be cruel!—but rather they will die out.[11]

**In your book, you cite French philosopher Diderot's *Supplement to the Voyage of Bougainville*. Do we know if Kant read that work, and where else he got his ideas about Tahiti? He cites Captain Cook's diary at one point.**

Diderot's *Supplement to the Voyage of Bougainville*, though written in 1772, was not published until after his death in 1796. And I believe that all of Kant's remarks about Tahitians predate 1796. However, Kant does cite Bougainville as well as Cook several times. Diderot's *Supplement* is an important counter-voice in Enlightenment debates about non-Europeans. Not all Enlightenment intellectuals were convinced that the West is the Best. But the *Supplement* has its own vices. Ultimately, it is more a projection of Diderot's own views than an accurate description of Tahitian culture.

**Kant talks about non-white races like the Tahitians dying or being 'wiped out' (*ausgerottet*) for lacking the skill, drive, and 'germs' (*Keime*) of whites.[12] Was he a social Darwinist ahead of his time or is his theory different?**

I see similarities as well as differences between Kantianism and Social Darwinism. One basic similarity is that both outlooks stress a version of 'only the strong survive'. But Kantianism has a theological dimension that is missing in Social Darwinism. On Kant's view, Providence has a plan for the human species, one that unfortunately grants more progress to some races than others.

**In an era in which many fear that the faculty of reason and rationality as standards of thought and ethical behaviour are being trampled on around the world, what part of Kant's ethics do you think stands the test of time?**

*Synkrētic*

I do think Kant's categorical imperative—particularly the formula of Humanity as an End in Itself (*'So act that you use humanity, in your own person as well as in the person of any other, always at the same time as an end, never merely as a means'*[13])—is a sound moral principle that has stood the test of time. Additionally, there are several aspects of the political side of Kant's practical philosophy—*e.g.*, the core commitment to human rights, a strong system of international law, and a federation of democratic states devoted to peace—that are sorely needed at present.

## Notes

1. Robert B. Louden and Günter Zöller (eds.), *Anthropology, History, and Education* (Cambridge: Cambridge University Press, 2007).
2. Immanuel Kant, *Lectures on Anthropology*, eds. Allen W. Wood and Robert B. Louden (Cambridge: Cambridge University Press, 2012).
3. Louden, *Kant's Impure Ethics: From Rational Beings to Human Beings* (New York: Oxford University Press, 2000).
4. Gabriele Rabel, *Kant* (Oxford: Clarendon Press, 1963).
5. See, *inter alia*, Jon M. Mikkelson, 'On the different races of human beings (1777)', in *The Idea of Race*, ed. Robert Bernasconi and Tommy Lee Lott (Indianapolis, Indiana: Hackett, 2000), 8-22.
6. 'Does the author really mean that if the happy inhabitants of Tahiti, never visited by more cultured nations, had been destined to live for thousands of centuries in their tranquil indolence, one could give a satisfying answer to the question why they exist at all, and whether it would not have been just as good to have this island populated with happy sheep and cattle as with human beings who are happy merely enjoying themselves?' Immanuel Kant, 'Review of J.G. Herder's *Ideas for the philosophy of the history of humanity. Parts 1 and 2* (1785)', transl. Allen W. Wood, in Robert B. Louden and Günter Zöller (eds.), *Anthropology, History, and Education* (Cambridge: Cambridge University Press, 2007), 142.
7. Louden, 'General Introduction', in *Anthropology, History, and Education*, 9.
8. Eunah Lee, 'Race and the Self-Defeating Character of Kant's Argument in Anthropology from a Pragmatic Point of View', in *Natur und Freiheit: Akten des XII. Internationalen Kant-Kongresses*, eds. Violetta L. Waibel, Margit Ruffing and David Wagner (Berlin: De Gruyter, 2018), 2737-2744.
9. Robert Bernasconi, 'Why Do the Happy Inhabitants of Tahiti Bother to Exist at All?', in *Genocide and Human Rights: A Philosophical Guide*, ed. John K. Roth (New York: Palgrave Macmillan, 2005), 139-148.

10  Louden, *Kant's Impure Ethics*, 212, note 92.
11  AA 25: 840; cf. *Lectures on Anthropology*, 274.
12  Louden, *Kant's Impure Ethics*, 212, note 92.
13  AA 4: 429.

STORIES

# King Buzzard*

*Bano Qudsia*†

TRANSLATED BY *Masood A. Raja*‡

*Translator's Note*

Bano Qudsia is, without a doubt, one of the leading figures of post-Partition Urdu literature in Pakistan. In her long career, she has published about thirty major works of fiction and many of her plays have been produced to critical acclaim for Pakistan television. Yet, despite her fame and accomplishments in Urdu literary circles, she remains unknown in the metropolitan cultures both in academia and in the popular realm due to a lack of English translations of her work. Published in 1981, *Raja Gidh*, her most important novel, was an instant success and received wide critical acclaim both in India and Pakistan. The purpose of this brief translated excerpt is to introduce the English-speaking readership to the richness and sophistication of Bano Qudsia's craft. It is almost impossible to

---

\* This is an excerpt from Pakistani novelist Bano Qudsia's *Raja Gidh* (1981) as translated from the Urdu by Masood A. Raja. This translation first appeared in the journal *Pakistaniaat*, Vol. 2, No. 1 (2010): 122-139.

† Bano Qudsia (1928-2017), a.k.a. Bano Aapa, was a prominent Pakistani writer known for her novel *Raja Gidh*. She earned a Masters in Urdu literature from Government College University in 1981 and lived in Lahore, Pakistan.

‡ Masood Ashraf Raja is Associate Professor of English and postcolonial literature at the University of North Texas. Dr Raja is editor of *Pakistaniaat* and earned his PhD from Florida State University. He lives in Denton, Texas, U.S.A.

convey the true beauty of her work and especially her mastery of Urdu idiom in English, but this attempt, imperfect as it may be, will be fruitful if it is able to at least introduce Qudsia's work to an English-speaking audience.

*Raja Gidh*, like all of Qudsia's work, is a complex novel. The novel's primary diegesis concerns the struggles of its main character, Qayum, while its secondary diegesis deals with the expulsion of the buzzards from the kingdom of birds. Thus, while Qayum goes through various stages of self-seeking in the main plot, the secondary plot provides the details of the trial of the King Buzzard. The main plot of the novel seeks to unravel the mystery of human madness. Qudsia suggests that there are two kinds of human madness: the constructive and the destructive, and it is the wisdom to know the difference between the two that makes one fully human. The main plot thus, through the interaction of its characters, charts the various reasons for human madness: unrequited love, unending search, fear of death, and so on.

The novel also deals with the question of right and wrong in terms of how we earn our living. Qudsia posits the idea that what we feed our children determines to some extent what kind of people they turn out to be. So, if the parents earn their living through corrupt means, the children end up paying the price. This concept was the main reason that the novel was selected to be one of the texts required for the Pakistani civil service exam. An aspect of the novel that garnered a lot of criticism is its treatment of human sexuality. For Urdu readers, Qudsia's exploration of human sexuality and its connection with human nature and spirit was quite shocking at first, but it is never used gratuitously and ultimately is seen as a component of the development of a spiritual self.

The following excerpts are intended to introduce Qudsia's work to a wider readership. I have tried to stay as close as possible to the original text and have only strayed from it at times to make the reading more accessible to the English-language reader.

*Synkrētic*

*Part One*
Evening

Unrequited Love

It was an October day—large, fluffy, and white like fresh popcorn. The previous few days had been as hot as a kiln, but this particular day was cool, expansive, and huge. Some days have the capacity to defy clocks and move at their own pace. It was the first day of our Masters class in sociology. The girls sat in the front row. *She was the best of those Chulistani gazelles.* Professor Suhail looked at her and said: 'Please introduce yourself.' We had all been speculating about her name, since the day of registration. She rose, rested her hand on her chair like a biker leaning against a motorcycle, and said:

'Sir, my name is Seemi Shah; I graduated from Kinniard College with a Bachelors in psychology and history.'

These were the first formal introductions. Farzana, Angela, Tayyiba, and Kausar had already introduced themselves. The first three came across as the kind of girls who had obtained their degrees by cramming pulp notes, and whose general knowledge and academic potential was mostly bookish. But Kausar Habib and Seemi Shah were the eyes of our class: glittering, bright, enticing. Kausar Habib, however, hesitated after impressing you; she would concede right when she was about to conquer. Her body and mind flickered like a light with intermittent power flow.

But Seemi Shah?

Well, she was a product of Gulberg's suburban society. This particular day she was clad in tight jeans and a white cotton *kurta*.[1] A necklace hung from her neck, touching her midriff. She had a canvas bag on her shoulder, which probably contained some money, lipstick, a tissue, a diary with certain phone numbers and people's birthdays inscribed in it. She probably also had a few expensive pens, which were useless for want of ink, so she borrowed others' ball-points to take her notes. Her hair was reddish black, and was ablaze on this glorious October day. She was sitting immediately in front of me, so close that, had I dared, I could have reached out and touched her finely tended hair, but the view of her bodice and her bra straps through her thin *kurta* terrified me far more than a loaded gun ever could have.

Aftab was the first in the boy's row to introduce himself after Seemi Shah. He stood up slowly, a replica of American film icons, illuminating, rhythmic, warm. He spoke in a baritone: 'I am Aftab Batt, and, as you already know, I am a graduate of this very college.'

Professor Suhail removed his glasses and said: 'Well, your classmates don't.'

On this Aftab first looked at the girl's row, then whirled to the boys like a discus thrower and said: 'I was the president of the student union last year; my majors were psychology and sociology. If I had not been so in love with myself and the movies, I could have probably topped the Bachelors exams. But I am not doleful about it. In fact, the girl who got the first position borrowed my notes to study. My reputation, however, is thankfully intact through God's grace and my fear of my parents.'

The whole class laughed. Someone yelled: 'Self trumpeter! Self trumpeter!'

Introductions continued. After five girls and fifteen boys had introduced themselves, the classroom air became musty with details of names and personal biographies. The class could have ended there, as people had started yawning, but Professor Suhail rose and picked up a piece of chalk from the table. He drew a large-headed, heavily moustached, thin-torsoed, big-booted figure on the board. Then he adorned this figure with square-framed glasses, gave him outstretched beseeching arms, and wrote beneath it: Dr Suhail; I will be teaching you sociology.

This comic-figure-drawing professor was only about five to six years older than us, but had the mastery of a lion trainer with a training whip hidden somewhere. He never mastered the functional aspects of teaching, but he was a master at mental judo. Ideological wrestling was his favourite sport, and he loved opening his students' skulls, and was good at closing them immediately if he found them vacant. He was also skilful at making the taciturn ones speak like parrots, while silencing the ones who went on incessantly like the radio. He spoke freely and encouraged freedom. Nothing shocked him. He knew a lot more than just sociology; in his presence, therefore, the air was free of academic pretensions and the students never stereotyped each other.

After drawing his self-portrait, Professor Suhail, while massaging the back of his neck, perched on the edge of the desk and said: 'I am not much older or more experienced than you, but as I am a Bachelor, books are still my first love. Books, so far, have been my main passion. You will certainly ask me some questions the answers to which I will not know. Unfortunately, I am too proud to accept anyone else's intellectual superiority. I therefore warn you that for as long as you are in my class, you should consider me your guru. You may not make much of my knowledge; it could sometimes be quite superficial. You might know more than me, but reminding me of my ignorance will be seriously harmful. It will cause my chest to constrict, I will shave off my whiskers, and my belt might become loose. Who would want me to suffer from such a drastic inferiority complex, raise your hand.'

No one raised a hand except Aftab.

'Why would you want me to suffer from an inferiority complex, Mr Aftab?'

'Sir, I think you already have an inferiority complex, so our saying so does not matter at all,' replied Aftab.

The whole class laughed, including Professor Suhail, who laughed the loudest. At this point an invisible triangle was drawn across the classroom space: Aftab held one point, Seemi the other, and Professor Suhail stood at the intercepting point of their gaze. Energy flowed amongst these three like the current through a circuit.

As the laughter subsided, Professor Suhail continued: 'I own an old motorcycle. If any male student needs it, just ask me for the keys. But whosoever does not return the bike at the promised time will forfeit the right to use it again. If a female student hails me at the bus stop for a lift, I will oblige, but would ask her to get off the bike the moment she tries to tell me where to turn. Now you all can report what you have to share with others.'

'Pen,' said someone form one corner.

'Bicycle, sometimes.'

'Tissues, always.'

'Notes, after the exams.'

'Lipstick,' said Seemi Shah.

'Flying kiss,' replied Aftab.

'Good, very good,' said Professor Suhail. 'Now we know that the GNP[2] of our sociology class is quite lofty, we can move on with aplomb. By the way, what do you think of the relation between the individual and society? Individual freedom is important, but do you think the society can survive if absolved of all its responsibilities?'

The professor's face had suddenly turned as old as his bike: the lecture had commenced.

Professor Suhail was expertly discussing the relationship between the individual and society. He often hit the ball into our court, which we returned using our best intellectual strokes. Pretty soon faces turned crimson, voices became intense, hands started chopping the air, and the girls, who until recently seemed to have been busy in a silent prayer, transformed into a group slashing at an ice slab with pikes. The conversation left the individual and society and ranged far and wide. We compared Sweden, Thailand, Rhodesia, Mexico, and Uganda, sometimes contemplating the powerlessness of individuals, or worrying over the plight of various societies.

Then Seemi Shah asked: 'Sir, do you think in an ideal society a person would commit suicide?'

The professor ran his fingers through his thick hair, and then threw the question back at the boys. Having found no useful comment he replied: 'In fact, suicide is a symptom. If one were to gauge a society with a social barometer, suicide would occur at its highest degree of pressure. But I am sorry to say, Miss Shah, that there is no such research community as yet in which we can perform this experiment. But it is believed that societal pressure causes madness, and madness becomes a cause of suicide.' He then went on to expound on Durkheim for quite some time.

We were all at an age when one develops a romantic and spiritual fondness for suicide. We argued about various causes of suicide: economic, social, individual, personal, and essential. As suicide was the effect and not the cause, the conversation soon shifted to mental ailments and insanity. We all agreed that insanity was the real cause of suicide; it was madness that impelled humans to take that last drastic step.

Angela had been silent throughout the discussion, while Farzana, Tayyiba, and Kausar, who had been previously arguing vehemently with Professor Suhail, went suddenly mute when the discussion turned to the cause instead of the effect.

Professor Suhail concluded: 'You all have clearly understood the relationship between the individual and the society and have drawn quite apt conclusions. Ms Farzana is right in suggesting that when the noose of society becomes overly tight around the individual's neck, the individual takes the tragic step of ending life before the time of natural death. Kausar has explained the reasons for suicide with the freshness of a true discovery. But now I invite you to contemplate beyond the act of suicide, which you all agree is the ultimate outcome of madness. Think about this aspect, not the suicide itself, but about madness; not the effect, but the cause. What is the real cause of madness? Remember, if madness is so baffling, then its cause must be even more extraordinary.'

Now, the boys jumped into the fray.

One suggested: 'There can be two reasons for madness: functional, caused by a birth defect, and psychological.'

'Look deeply for any reasons besides this,' said Professor Suhail.

Aftab had not said a word until then. This Kashmiri boy had remained seated like a decorated birthday gift in its white wrappings. We learned later that when it came to academic discussions, he never wasted words: where a smile sufficed, he would avoid using a word, and if a word was enough, he would not waste a sentence, and he preferred brevity over prolixity. He usually spoke in points. He would count his responses on his fingers, one, two, three. He rarely crossed number three; but what he said this day was probably his longest articulation during his entire Masters career.

He rose and stretched his hands outwards like a cross. His arms were covered with hair, like thick golden grass. The light from the window struck his brown eyes and made them sparkle like glittering honey. He looked like an athlete carrying the Olympic torch: beautiful, pure, hallowed. It was at this moment that Seemi made the mistake of looking at him, and was driven mad.

'Madness is caused by unfulfilled desires, sir,' he said. 'These desires,' he continued 'are caused by the social taboos present in every culture. In the cultures where one can't marry one's cousins, the unrequited love of one's cousin becomes the cause of insanity.'

'Thank you for borrowing from Freud,' Seemi slashed at him in her scissor-like English.

'*Madam*, I have not borrowed this from the Repression Theory; I am speaking of Mir Taqi Mir's[3] madness, Farhad's madness.[4] Professor Suhail exposed us to one aspect of madness: suicide and death. I am speaking of the other side of lunacy; the kind of madness that is divine, sacred; the kind of madness that drives one to conquer Mount Everest, or dig a canal of milk.'[5]

'Sit down Farhad *sahib*,'[6] yelled a boy from one corner. Aftab gave him a fiery look and sat down.

'That's a point,' said Professor Suhail, his eyes suddenly luminous. 'So, we have reached a conclusion' he continued, 'that madness has two kinds, positive and negative. Good, very good. Now, your assignment for this month is to share with me at least one reason for human madness. This reason cannot only be biological, or environmental; it should be completely innovative; it could be some spiritual or mystical idea, but new. The one who comes up with the most insane answer will get the most points.'

The class was in turmoil.

'Madness is caused by only one thing: environment, environment...' said someone from a corner.

'No, it's biological...' yelled another.

'Repression, sir...'

*Synkrētic*

'Agree or disagree, but madness is caused by only one thing: *Ishq-e-lahaasi!* Unrequited love, unrequited love, unrequited love,' shouted Aftab, while standing on his chair.

'Order! Order,' roared Professor Suhail. 'Friends, my pay increment is at stake here; if you make such a racket, someone will report me to the chancellor, and I will be posted to Muzaffargarh.'

The discussion soon became a rudderless ship. One student talked about group marriages and use of hashish, then someone mentioned the Western moral decay and the race problem. Everything became worth a shot: the North African refugee problem in Sweden, Red Indians and their shamans, colonialism and the problems of democracy, Japan's industrial excellence, the ever-unravelling Russian communism *etc.*, *etc.* But Seemi Shah was speechless—she had been vanquished by Aftab's idea of unrequited love.

She was a flower of Gulberg; she had studied at Convent schools. In her free time she enjoyed Western music, read *Newsweek* and *Time*, watched American TV shows. Her wardrobe included only a few Shalwar *kurtas*; for her looks, she relied on shampoo, hair spray, colognes, and perfumes. She had never had to wash herself using a mug and a bucket of water; this back-brush-wielding, shower-using daughter of Gulberg was smitten by the inner-city Kashmiri boy, exactly when he was busy announcing: '*Ishq-e-lahaasi!* Unrequited love! Unrequited love!'

They had previously exchanged some surreptitious looks. But during this third period, their eyes first became filled with wonder, and then with recognition and finally with understanding. After the class, they both rose in a trance, and, as if under a spell, exited the classroom side by side. Outside, Seemi quietly mounted Aftab's motorcycle. Aftab never raised an eyebrow. Like in a movie scene, they both slowly faded out on the road.

Three people jolted my being on this day. Aftab, with his Hellenic bearing, was one of them. If he had not been in the class, then probably I could have been the most popular in the class. This induced a special jealousy and ill-will in my heart for him.

*King Buzzard*

The second shock came from Professor Suhail. Previously, I had been accustomed to professors who taught from textbook notes. They all had been teaching from these notes from the beginning of their careers and would probably retire with the same knowledge; there was no chance of their intellectual growth. They were stuck with the ideas they had started with, and there wasn't much chance for change.

In high school, I was in the care of Master Ghulam Rasul. His beard, his booming voice, and his table were immutable. He carried a cane that he placed on the table the moment he entered the class. His long beard shone with hair colouring. He used to curse us the same way the policemen addressed felons. The volume control in his voice was broken, so he always used the highest notes. As we could not remove his staff, we took our revenge on the table instead. We had carved hundreds of curses on the four legs of the table with our compasses. But, despite our abuse, the table never left the classroom. Master Ghulam Rasul was quite immovable, too. If he declared that the War of Independence had happened in 1647 CE, then so it was, and no reference to venerable history books could change his mind. Because of his influence, his students were mostly cowards, mean, and unkind to the elderly. He could not accept any criticism of the Mughal kings. All of them, from Babar to Bahadur Shah Zafar, were his heroes. Any criticisms of the Mughals incensed him, and as he could not convince us with his arguments, he drowned us out with his loud, booming voice.

In ninth grade I chanced upon *Tuzk-e-Jahangiri*.[7] I shared the details of the book with my classmates frequently. Knowing master Ghulam Rasul's veneration of the Mughals, but being young and arrogant, and wanting to impress my classmates further, I decided to ask a question. 'Master Jee,' I said, 'have you read *Tuzk-e-Jahangiri*?'

'I read it when you were still pissing in your pants. Sit down and don't try to impress us with your knowledge!' he replied.

'Master Jee,' I ventured again.

'What?'

*Synkrētic*

'There are events recorded in the book suggesting that Jahangir wasn't all that compassionate.'

Master Ghulam Rasul smashed his chalk on the table.

'He married Noor Jehan. Isn't that compassion? Why would a king marry a divorcee? Was there any dearth of virgins? Tell me if this was compassion or not?' He yelled.

Master and I had two different ways of measuring compassion.

'Master Jee, he had one criminal immured in a goat skin and then had the skin sewed shut,' I said.

'Well, he was a criminal, not an innocent. Punishment is always for good. Now, when I punish you, does it benefit me or you? Punishments are for the good of the felon,' he roared.

'But Master Jee, how could the one who got sewn up in a goat skin benefit from the punishment?'

'Sit down! You argue like your older brother. We will talk about Jahangir the Great when you grow a moustache,' he concluded.

He always added, like in Alexander the Great, 'the Great' to every Mughal king's name, and as I was always quite shy about my non-existent moustache, I sat down immediately. But that first attempt at showing off my knowledge started a rebellion in my heart.

That most teachers are usually quite conventional in their ideas is the greatest misfortune of the teaching profession. The teachers love discipline, middle class values, and hardworking students. They teach about unusual people and their accomplishments, people who were nonconformists. Hence, being common themselves, the teachers teach about people whose level of thought they themselves don't possess. They thrive in making children normal, common, while their educational materials incite the students to be unusual, uncommon. The dropouts do not belong in the school, but they are always lectured about the people who themselves were school dropouts. Every Ghulam Rasul tries to teach normatively to students using works about the geniuses of history, and this is the great tragedy of education: the works of special people in the hands of the ordinary. It was because of this disparity in our educational system that I could never grow tall inside, even though outwardly I had grown taller. Inside, I was like a Bonsai tree, centuries old, yet a pygmy.

I was careful to the point of being impractical. It was all right on an intellectual level, but in real life I was like a lost dog. I needed a guru who could stretch me to make me as tall as him, but I ran into yet another Master Ghulam Rasul after high school.

I met him during the first year of college. Professor Tanvir always smoked imported cigarettes, dressed in spotless three-piece suits, and wore thick power glasses. He was quite erudite, and I was impressed by the depth of his learning. As my early experience was rural, I preferred the feudal system, but he was an ardent socialist. Theoretically, he attributed all social ills to the uneven distribution of wealth. I quite took to him during my first year, but he turned out to be yet another Master Ghulam Rasul. He was only an academic socialist. His lifestyle was completely feudal, and he could not accept any criticism of his views or his lifestyle.

If any student pointed out a disparity in his views and his real life, he denied them the same freedom of speech that he idealised. It was during the week before the final BA exams, when he was proving his open-mindedness by allowing us to smoke in class, that I asked him a question.

'Sir, there is something I wanted to ask.'

'Oh, keep smoking, we are friends, and ask your question' he said.

'Sir, you tell us every day that capitalism is the root cause of Third World poverty, then why don't you sell your car and buy a cheap motorcycle?' I asked. I was young then and did not know of the incongruity between people's words and deeds.

Professor Tanvir's face turned red. Restraining his anger he said: 'This is a totally personal question, sit down. You rural folks lack manners; idiot, if I sell my car then how will I get to college?'

I felt slighted, and could not let go of the discussion. So just to annoy him further, I said: 'On a bicycle, sir, just like all the other people.'

'This is the space age, you idiot; time is valuable and you want me to revert to a bike?'

*Synkrētic*

'But sir, China is in the space age, too, but people there...'

'You want an intellectual to ride a bike, while the businessmen and mill owners and the nouveau riche travel in their shiny cars? We have carved out a place in this society after years of hard work and struggle and you want us to give it up!' said Professor Tanvir.

'But sir, according to your beliefs society should be classless, so there is no fear of losing one's place.'

Now the professor was foaming at the mouth and he flailed his arms, shouting, 'Sit down, sit down. A frog's mind cannot contain Marx's ideas. First learn how to tie your necktie, then we will talk about these things.'

I hid my necktie behind my palm and sat down. Professor Tanvir did not know how to open minds; he was incapable of providing the kind of education that could reduce the difference between words and deeds.

But Professor Suhail wasn't like an immutable sealed parchment. He was like a slate: you could write, erase, and write again. I was surprised at his love of books; books had been my passion too for a long time. But the books had driven me away from the lighter side of life; I had learned that those who loved books forgot about the lighter aspects of life, and became serious priests in the habit of hitting others with the staff of their learned ideas.

Professor Suhail was different and interesting. All my life had been scarred by Ghulam Rasuls, so I was fascinated by this childlike, simple, and well-humoured professor. The introductory lesson made me disillusioned about my earlier education. I got bored with Buddha's *Dhamphada*[8] and modern parapsychology. I wished to be a simple slate, so that I could erase what had been inscribed on it earlier to write Professor Suhail's assignments with new insight, according to his expectations. Even though I had not yet started his assignment, I was already afraid of disappointing him.

After succumbing to Aftab's splendour and Professor Suhail's learning, my third genuflection was to Seemi Shah. It was probably a victory of urban culture over the rural. I had never before seen such a completely urban girl. She transported me to the world of advertisements, of plane fights through clouds. Her accent, dress, manners, and smell all revealed that she was more refined. Now, my pride incited me to break her and drag her to my rural home where she would become a complete village girl. So that her days and nights would be spent, like my mother, churning milk, plying the spinning wheel, and cooking vegetables in large earthen pots. Maybe every man desires to force a woman from her own chosen path to a course of his choosing.

But Aftab had already left with Seemi on his motorcycle. At that very instant, he was probably giving her, in Urdu, her first lecture about the history of inner-city Lahore.

\*\*\*

Some people say that the region of Potohar, made up of arid, second-rate hills the natives call Pabbian, was once a puissant blue ocean. Then a Yogi, who meditated upon its beaches for three hundred years, taught the ocean to hide. Each wave returned back to the Arabian sea, singing its hymn, *malagan, palagan*, laying bare the submerged barren hills. The geological aspects of these hills still reflect the water marks of the ancient ocean.

Some others say that Potohar was once a thick jungle. The trees in this jungle were so tall and thickly intertwined that even the streams running through it got lost, and the sunrays never reached far enough to create multi-coloured whirlpools in their waters. The birds roamed this jungle freely, and even the night owls could see during the day. Then one night a haunting wind descended from the moon and devastated the forest and dried up the streams. This forest thrived centuries ago in the first age of human civilisation, a civilisation that had all the knowledge that we now possess.

It was in this first age that the humans travelled to Mars and Jupiter, and invented atomic bombs. When the bowstring of civilisation was stretched to its limit, the humans destroyed God's world with their bombs and this forest became a wasteland.

This story is of the specific time from the first age of human civilisation when humans had not yet used their bombs. There was great fear amongst the dwelling places of animals about this new human innovation. Hence, a conference of the birds was called in the jungle. So many birds came to attend this conference that there wasn't enough room for them to perch.

From Hind Sind came the grey-winged birds in droves. From the hills of Khasi came the red-tailed bulbul and the emerald green pigeon whose orange underwings dazzled the eyes of the beholder. The Bajanga from Kathmandu and the eagles from Tibet arrived, having camped several times during their long flight. Not only the African partridges, moorhens and nightingales made their way to the meeting, but even the birds of prey suspended their activities and flew from America and Australia to the meeting place. Even the Shikra, Baz,[9] and eagles, residents of Central Asia and Russian Turkestan, reached the meeting in the company of the birds of Pamir. The crow, Mynah,[10] quails, woodpeckers, chakoors,[11] and sparrows were natives and their collective votes counted, but their individual opinions were not considered worthy, while the hook-billed, high-flying birds pranced around like the white races. From the basin of the River Gagahr and Chatranji came the latoras, chandols,[12] and goghais[13] flying magnificently in battle formations like fighter planes. The gold-backs, neelkanths[14] and hudhuds[15] chose the tree stumps as their perches. The doves, cuckoos, and chandols were not much interested in the conference, for them it did not matter much if the humans destroyed the world, and had come just to gossip with the denizens of the forest, but were shocked to learn the seriousness of the situation.

A few days before the conference, the air was filled with the disparate opinions of the birds. Everyone was waiting for the President, without whom the meeting could not commence. The reconnaissance party returned from Mount Everest, reporting that they had combed all the mountains—Dhulidar, Nangaparbat, K2, Kanchnaga—but had found no signs of Huma.[16] It was assumed that the world was awaiting the arrival of some powerful king, and Huma was on a VIP tour to help the forces of the universe choose this king. This supposed tour also became a subject of gossip amongst the birds. Some carnivore birds thought that the end of the world was near, and that it would be brought by human hands. They thought the world needed a pure being to save it from the disaster, and Huma, instead of choosing the king, was searching for this Messiah. Some other birds thought that Huma had become mystical-minded, and having announced the vice-regency of man to humans, had now given up and become a recluse, for every caliph he chose had become a tyrant instead. Huma, thus, had lost hope in humanity and had vowed not to fly over human heads again.

The Owl Jati, who never interfered in others' business, did not agree with this opinion. They thought that Huma, because of his narcissistic delusions, had never cared about God's will, and he could only guess the desires of a few humans. Therefore, whosoever Huma chose as the king became a downfall for his people. The night owls were more interested in observation than speech, and did not express much and waited patiently for Mr President's arrival.

Even though the Owl Jati leaders had conversed about this within their inner circles, the crows, the inquisitive bastards—an art they had learned from humans—got wind of it. Thus the round-eyed owls' secret was spread to the whole jungle, and the whole jungle resonated with rumours. The crows had always considered Huma a circus clown who had been eternally stubborn and often wrong. Thus, when Huma remained absent for a long time, the birds got tired of waiting. The crows were rightly incensed, for they had long lost the habit of residing in the forest; they were, rather, more accustomed to sitting on the house walls eavesdropping on housewives, and this absence of human contact was troubling them. So, every now and then, a few wise, cunning, and cowardly crows would surround the smaller birds and incite them thusly: 'Huma is an eternal fool who keeps choosing the kings on the earth. Brothers, every human is a king, whether he sleeps in the manger or on a throne. Huma is stupid and does not understand that every human considers himself the Best-of-all-Beings; those who wear the crown of pride, what need is there to make them kings?'

The Peacocks, with their tails spread, kept rehearsing the welcome dance all over the jungle: they were happy for being part of the reception committee. The crows used a different language with the peacocks. 'Huma is a different matter; only he will suit the Presidential chair; nothing can be done without Huma as the president.'

The empty Presidential chair prompted a search for an alternate to Huma. It was discovered that the mountain from where the ocean had receded—where one could still find oyster shells, snails, scorpions, fish skeletons, and the remains of other sea creatures—was the abode of a Simurgh.[17] No one knew of his exact age. Some birds insisted that he had been a refugee on Baba Noah's ark. Others speculated that he had always lived in the sacred areas—the ones that the Isrælis are now trying to annex—to derive energy from the mosque of Aqsa.[18] The old sea turtles insisted that the Simurgh had lived in the Mediterranean desert, which later was filled with the waters of the Mediterranean ocean.

The Simurgh spent the whole night gazing at the moon to absorb the lunar energy, and spent his days sunbathing in the desert. The dove opined that it was because of Simurgh's powers that Potohar became a jungle: if the lunar energy had not appeared in the Simurgh, not even a single wave of water would have receded from Potohar. It was the magnetic energy of lunar power that had forced the waters to rise and fall back into the Arabian sea.

The reclusive Simurgh hated the noise, and the company of the denizens of the forest distressed him. He was accustomed to living in the uninhabited lands and eating only what was absolutely necessary to sustain life. But the search party finally found him and having beseeched him in the name of his experience, intelligence, and knowledge convinced him to preside at the conference. Simurgh arrived during the latter part of a full moon night. A few moments before his arrival, the sky was shaken with tree-bending winds. The storm-loving birds rose up to reach the skies, while the timid ones hung helplessly from the tree branches. The lightning struck and the land trembled; the bolts of lightning transformed the night into day. Just as the birds were struck dumb by the ear-shattering noise of thunder and lightning, Simurgh alighted on the fourteen-century old banyan tree. The storm subsided as soon as he took his place on the tree. The forest went quiet and the banyan tree glowed in fluorescent light. As soon as the Simurgh flapped his

## King Buzzard

wings to accept his new responsibility, the jungle rumbled with a noise like that of thundering cannons, and the birds feared the coming of an earthquake.

'Why have you called such a huge conference?' asked the Simurgh.

An aggressive Kite left her group and moved briskly forward to answer the question. 'Master, we have a serious and complex problem. As you might have noticed, the human of today has become civilised for the first time. He has, with his inventive knowledge, travelled to Mars and Jupiter, but there is also something in human instinct that is a cause of his destruction—madness. It is because of this madness that he has created weapons that can destroy the earth in minutes along with all who live on this sphere. O King of the Birds, we have noticed that some of the birds are also becoming subjects of this madness. We fear that their madness, well, could ultimately become the destruction of the world of birds.'

'Who is mad, who is mad?' asked all the birds.

The Kite continued. 'We don't care about the details, Master…but no bird has ever gone mad until now. If the birds start going insane like the jackals and the foxes, then what will happen to the life in the jungle…the main point is that this madness, like that of the humans, might destroy the world of the birds.'

'Who amongst us is mad? Tell, tell!' cried all the birds.

'Friends,' the Kite continued, 'we don't want to blame anyone, but these days the Gidh[19] Jati has been known to do strange things. For years we have noticed that they eat to the fullest, vomit, and eat again. And in the moonlit nights, they leave the green forests and run in the arid, barren lands like sailboats running against the winds.'

All the birds suddenly looked at the vultures, who were sitting with their beaks tucked under their wings, like so many amnesiacs.

The kite hissed again: 'They must be punished, Your Honour, or else we, who resemble them, would be disgraced because of them.'

Simurgh flicked his fluorescent light thrice as an announcement. The whole jungle fell silent. Then he said: 'This isn't as simple as you state. First, we need to know if the vulture Jati's madness is really of any danger to the bird community; secondly, we must know the real reason for this madness. If it is essential to their being, then we are helpless, for then it is between them and their maker.

The kites were not interested in discussion; they just desired the banishment of their vulture look-alikes. The eagles and hawks were troubled at this likeness, too, but the kites were hasty and aggressive. The same kite said again, 'Master, when humans went mad, no one cared about it, and now they are suffering the consequences of it. If we do not pay attention to this today, then the jungle community will vanish from the earth. Our personal grievance is unimportant, we can deal with it, but it is also an issue of everyone's survival. Don't you all want to live, to survive?'

The birds were not really interested in a just decision, but the word survival caused an uproar. 'Expel! Expel! Expel!' they shouted.

This terrified the dust-coloured finches who had until then sat quietly, disinterested.

The Surkhab,[20] as the legal advisor, said the pacifying words: 'Brothers,' he said 'this problem is not as simple as you think. We have all the birds of the world here, so let us decide with a majority vote.'

The jungle reverberated with yet another uproar: 'Banishment is the punishment for madness: Expulsion! Expulsion!'

A wisened old Kite rose from his group and said: 'Master, send them to the human world. They are building the bombs that will obliterate all life. When those crazies erase their own seed, let the vultures be a part of it!'

The woodpecker, feeling a surge of compassion, said hesitantly, '*Sain*,[21] all of us birds sometimes visit the human cities, but always return. The humans do impact us but not permanently. But if we banish the vultures completely to the human world then we will be responsible for their sins, for they will certainly learn evil from humans like envy and jealousy.'

The crows interrupted, 'Where is it written that human company causes envy and jealousy? Human is God's vice regent, after all. Such talk does not suit us birds.'

## King Buzzard

The woodpecker, finding the mynah in his favour looked to her and said, 'Why don't *you* say something?'

Mynah flapped her wings to gain everybody's attention, and said: 'The first human madness happened when Cain killed Abel. The crow saw human helplessness and alighted from the skies to teach Cain how to hide the body of his brother. Look at human pettiness, for they, instead of thanking the crow for his kindness, denigrated him and have always tried to enslave the birds with their intelligence. And when people of Cain feasted, they slaughtered wild animals, eating the meat themselves and throwing the bones everywhere. The dogs and cats, seeing this plenty, left their clans and settled in human habitations; they ate their fill and buried the rest in the sand, became victims of greed. This is a long story, Master, very long …humans might be the Best-of-all-the-Beings, but we cannot trust them; their company has never been beneficial for birds and animals.

The parrot, being the mynah's rival, interrupted and said: 'If human company causes madness, and engenders envy, jealousy, and greed, then how come the donkey isn't so, even though he is man's oldest companion?'

Mynah objected, 'Tell me, how have the humans treated the donkey for all his loyalty, and kind-heartedness? How much is he burdened by the humans, and whenever they need to label someone foolish, they call him a donkey. The humans, when they cannot profit form the milk-giving animals, sell them to the butcher. Let's not talk about humans, friends, or this discussion will be endless.'

The Kite, alarmed at this turn of the argument, interrupted and said, 'It is pointless to discuss the profit and loss of the case. Sentence and expel! Sentence and expel!'

The Cuckoo implored, 'Think, Justices. The Vulture will never return from the land of humans. We have an old relationship with the vultures; they have lived here in the same trees with us; how would they reform and rehabilitate in the company of men? How will it cure them?'

'You worry about the cure,' interrupted the Kite, 'we are worried that this madness will infect the whole forest. Then what will we

*Synkrētic*

do?' The kites did not care about the discussion; they just wanted to hear the sentence.

But all the birds, having heard the Cuckoo's words, sat musing, with their neck outstretched.

Seeing this, the quick-eyed Kite spoke again: 'This discussion has enlightened us partially, but has not allayed our fears completely. We demand that the Vulture nation be excommunicated and expelled from the forest. Then, if they want to relate with the fishes or the humans, it is up to them; they will not be considered a part of the world of birds.'

Upon this, the black stork rose and, while standing on one leg, said: 'It's not my place to speak in the company of such worthies, but will it be odd to ask the vulture to speak?'

The fluorescent light flickered thrice, and the Simurgh asked: 'Raja Gidh,[22] what say you? Do you admit that you are unlike other birds? Do you suffer from fits of madness?'

Raja Gidh alighted from the tree branches and ambled forward to speak: 'Yes, Master. On the moonlit nights, I fall off tall, canopied trees. I lose self-control. I do not recognise my own kin. Then I wander on paths that lead nowhere.'

'Why are you compelled to act like this? No other bird suffers from such insanity.'

'He has confessed! Confessed!' yelled the kite group. 'When the foxes howl in the agony of madness,' continued Raja Gidh 'we lose ourselves, Master…we do not understand this madness. We know we are guilty, but what causes this, we do not know. We will be thankful if someone could enlighten us about it.'

Upon this the Najdi bulbul spoke, 'Friends, I am an inhabitant of deserts, my throat is imbued with the songs of the caravans, and my chest is crimson with the blood of human love. I have witnessed humans for centuries, and I can tell you that the cause of Vulture's madness can be traced to human insanity. Human madness resides in an energy, which if stemmed can shatter the self to pieces.'

Owl, the most learned of all the birds, was suddenly attentive: 'What kind of energy? Mechanical energy, atomic energy, electrical energy, potential or kinetic energy, sound or light energy?'

The Bulbul swelled her red chest and said, 'All these energies combined make the human power.'

Everyone looked at the Bulbul with wide-eyed wonder.

'Human,' the Bulbul continued 'is driven mad because of this very energy. Understand my worthies, when the energy is contained, it breaks the very vessel in which it is trapped.'

'How do you know? How? How?' yelled the birds.

'I am a resident of Najd. When my Sheikh travelled for trade, he carried me with him in a golden cage. Once, a *sanyasi*[23] from Benares revealed to me the true cause of human madness.'

'Tell! Reveal the sealed secret!'

'The human power lies in sexual energy; unlike animals and the birds, humans do not use this sexual energy for procreation alone. They rather keep this dark steed of energy restrained. This powerful restrained steed of energy helps them in traversing the long distance of the physical and the metaphysical worlds. Those who can control this wild steed attain absolute wisdom, but if they sit loosely in the saddle, then they fall and are called insane. The knowledge of the physical world results in poetry, painting, music, and art. But if the emphasis is metaphysical, and the energy strong, then the humans touch the apex of awareness. If this power is withdrawn, they commit suicide. If the love is unrequited, then the horse drags the rider and humans become insane. People tie them up, stone them for their madness. This unrequited love is the true cause of human madness!'

The phosphorous light flickered thrice, and the Simurgh asked: 'But what has human madness got to do with the Gidh Jati?'

The Bulbul replied, 'Knowledge always travels from known to the unknown. Can't we extrapolate from our knowledge of the human madness to suggest that Raja Gidh probably possess the same power and energy?'

'You mean the energy of unrequited love?' asked the Surkhab.

'Yes, somehow, he seems to have gained the same power.'

'Under the oath of God-given sustenance, tell us if you possess this energy?' asked the Simurgh.

## *Synkrētic*

Raja Gidh fluttered his wings and said: 'Master, I need time; I am not aware of this secret. If you grant me some time, I can consult with my brethren and then apprise you of what we discover.'

Upon this, the Simurgh extinguished the phosphate lamp. The clouds thundered and lightning flashed, the jungle turned fluorescent white. The meeting was adjourned till the next gathering. The birds started leaving in small groups, and the jungle faded out amidst the whispering hisses of snakes.

## Notes

1 *Kurta*: A loose, cotton shirt worn by men and women in South Asia and around the world.
2 *GNP*: The gross national product or gross national income measures a country's total earnings.
3 *Mir Taqi Mir's madness*: a leading 18th century Urdu poet known for his melancholy tone and themes of madness.
4 *Farhad's madness*: A reference to the Persian poem of Shireen and Farhad, or Khosrow and Shirin in the original by Azerbaijani poet Nizami Ganjavi (1141–1209), in which the lovelorn Farhad descends into madness.
5 *Dig a canal of milk*: This is a reference to the Persian love poem of 'Shireen and Farhad' in which Farhad is given the impossible task of digging a canal and then filling it with milk in order for him to be able to court Shireen.
6 *Sahib*: An honorific Arabic title meaning 'companion', roughly equivalent to 'sir'.
7 *Tuzk-e-Jahangiri*: the posthumous autobiography of Mughal emperor Nur al-Din Muhammad Jahangir (1569-1627).
8 *Dhammapada*: one of the canonical works of Buddhist scripture, which consists of the Buddha's sayings.
9 *Baz*: the *bāz* is a diurnal bird of prey which often appears in traditional Persian literature.
10 *Mynah*: also known as a myna, this small bird is a member of the starling family and native to South Asia.
11 *Chakoors*: the chukar is partridge native to Asia that is found in India and was introduced in Australia.
12 *Chandols*: Bodal chandol is the Punjabi name for the crested lark (*Galerida cristata*) found in northwest India.
13 *Goghais*: Likely Jerdon's babblers (*Chrysomma altirostre*), known in Pakistan's Sindh province as Jorden Ki Ghoghais.

14 *Neelkanths*: the Hindi name of the Indian roller bird, which is considered an auspicious symbol of God.
15 *hudhuds*: also known as hoopoes, these small birds with a golden crest on their heads appear in the Quran.
16 *Huma*: the character is likely named after the mythical Huma bird of Persian literature, one akin to the *Simurgh*.
17 *Simurgh*: a mythical bird found in Persian literature as well as Kurdish, Georgian, Armenian, and other cultures.
18 *Mosque of Aqsa*: the Al-Aqsa or Qibli Mosque is an important Muslim holy site in the Old City of Jerusalem.
19 *Gidh*: the Urdu word for vulture.
20 *Surkhab*: a brightly coloured fowl found in Asia, also known as the Chinese golden pheasant (*Chrysolophus pictus*).
21 *Sain*: an honorific title signalling one's profound respect for its recipient, also meaning 'teacher'.
22 *Raja Gidh*: 'Raja' meaning king in Hindi, this character and the book's title mean 'King Vulture' or 'King Buzzard'.
23 *Sanyasi*: A *sannyasi* is a Hindu religious ascetic or holy man who has renounced the world.

# Bahloo the moon*

*Peter Hippai, Hippitha,
Matah, Barahgurrie, Beemunny,*[†]
*Katie Langloh Parker,*[‡] *Jane Singleton*[§]

I. Bahloo the moon, and the *daens*\*\*

Bahloo the moon looked down at the earth one night, when his light was shining quite brightly, to see if anyone was moving. When the earth people were all asleep was the time he chose for playing with his three dogs. He called them dogs, but the earth people called them snakes, the death adder, the black snake, and the tiger snake. As he looked down onto the earth, with his three dogs beside him, Bahloo saw about a dozen *daens*,[1] or black fellows, crossing a creek.

---

\* These oral history accounts were collected and published in K. Langloh Parker, *Australian Legendary Tales: Folklore of the Noongahburrahs as told to the Piccaninnies* (Melbourne: D. Nutt, 1896). This work is in the public domain.

† Peter Hippai (c. 1835-1904) was a Yuwaalaraay Senior Law Man of the Noongahburrah or Narran tribe and stockman whom Katie Langloh Parker cites as an oral history source. Hippitha, Matah, Barahgurrie, and Beemunny, also from the same area near the Narran River which crosses Australia's Queensland-New South Wales border, are also sources.

‡ Katie Langloh Parker (1856-1940) was a South Australian writer and ethnographer. She notated the Yuwaalaraay language and oral history while living on Bangate Station near Goodooga, New South Wales, Australia.

§ Jane Singleton is a journalist who worked at the *ABC*, *The Age*, *The Financial Times*, and *The Economist*. She holds a Bachelor of Arts from the University of Melbourne and has taught journalism. She lives in Sydney, Australia.

\*\* Langloh Parker, *Australian Legendary Tales*, 8-11.

He called to them saying, 'Stop, I want you to carry my dogs across that creek.' But the black fellows, though they liked Bahloo well, did not like his dogs, for sometimes when he had brought these dogs to play on the earth, they had bitten not only the earth dogs but their masters; and the poison left by the bites had killed those bitten. So, the black fellows said, 'No, Bahloo, we are too frightened; your dogs might bite us. They are not like our dogs, whose bite would not kill us.'

Bahloo said, 'If you do what I ask you, when you die you shall come to life again, not die and stay always where you are put when you are dead. See this piece of bark. I throw it into the water.' And he threw a piece of bark into the creek. 'See it comes to the top again and floats. That is what would happen to you if you would do what I ask you: first under when you die, then up again at once. If you will not take my dogs over, you foolish *daens*, you will die like this,' and he threw a stone into the creek, which sank to the bottom. 'You will be like that stone, never rise again, *Wombah daens*!'

But the black fellows said, 'We cannot do it, Bahloo. We are too frightened of your dogs.'

'I will come down and carry them over myself to show you that they are quite safe and harmless.' And down he came, the black snake coiled round one arm, the tiger snake round the other, and the death adder on his shoulder, coiled towards his neck. He carried them over. When he had crossed the creek he picked up a big stone, and he threw it into the water, saying, 'Now, you cowardly *daens*, you would not do what I, Bahloo, asked you to do, and so forever you have lost the chance of rising again after you die. You will just stay where you are put, like that stone does under the water, and grow, as it does, to be part of the earth. If you had done what I asked you, you could have died as often as I die, and have come to life as often as I come to life. But now you will only be black fellows while you live, and bones when you are dead.'

Bahloo looked so cross, and the three snakes hissed so fiercely, that the black fellows were very glad to see them disappear from their sight behind the trees. The black fellows had always been frightened of Bahloo's dogs, and now they hated them, and they said, 'If we could get them away from Bahloo we would kill them.' And thenceforth, whenever they saw a snake alone they killed it. But Bahloo only sent more, for he said, 'As long as there are black fellows there shall be snakes to remind them that they would not do what I asked them.'

II. Mooregoo the mopoke, and Bahloo the moon*

Mooregoo the mopoke[2] had been camped away by himself for a long time. While alone he had made a great number of boomerangs, nullah-nullahs,[3] spears, neilahmans,[4] and opossum rugs. Well had he carved the weapons with the teeth of opossums, and brightly had he painted the inside of the rugs with coloured designs, and strongly had he sewn them with the sinews of opossums, threaded in the needle made of the little bone taken from the leg of an emu. As Mooregoo looked at his work he was proud of all he had done.

One night Bahloo the moon came to his camp, and said: 'Lend me one of your opossum rugs.'

'No. I lend not my rugs.'

'Then give me one.'

'No, I give not my rugs.'

Looking round, Bahloo saw the beautifully carved weapons, so he said, 'Then give me, Mooregoo, some of your weapons.'

'No, I give, never, what I have made, to another.'

Again Bahloo said, 'The night is cold. Lend me a rug.'

'I have spoken,' said Mooregoo. 'I never lend my rugs.'

Bahloo said no more, but went away, cut some bark and made a *dardurr*[5] for himself. When it was finished and he safely housed in it, down came the rain in torrents. And it rained without ceasing until the whole country was flooded. Mooregoo was drowned. His weapons floated about and drifted apart, and his rugs rotted in the water.

---

\* Langloh Parker, *Australian Legendary Tales*, 68-69.

### III. How Bahloo warns of rain*

It is to the legend of 'Mooregoo the mopoke, and Bahloo the moon' that we owe a black fellow's reason for a halo round the moon. Ever since the storm in that legend when Bahloo built himself a *dardurr*, he has done so before rain. Seeing a halo the Blacks say, 'Bahloo has built his *dardurr*, there will be rain.'

### IV. How Bahloo warns of frost†

I learnt that when the sun, as it sometimes does in summer, goes down like a fiery red ball, it is the reflection of wattle gum on it that makes it so bright. After such a sunset, if [the Noongahburrah tribe] go out for gum, they are certain to find quantities; they say. The gum they melt in water, making it into a half liquid jelly which they eat with relish, and which they say has great strengthening properties. [They say] that when the moon looks very yellow after it has risen on a winter's evening, it is a sign of frost. 'The Meamei[6] have told Bahloo they will send frost tonight. He is going to keep himself warm; look at his bright fire,' they say.

### V. An excerpt from Jane Singleton, *What Katie Did*‡

Katie Langloh Parker was a white woman who notated the Aboriginal language Euahlayi[7] and collected the *Legends from the Noongahburrahs* in the later decades of the 19th century. But her publication of the *Noongahburrah Legends* is controversial. There have been both critical and supportive critiques of her work, but little on the woman herself who accomplished something extraordinary as a 19th century squatter's wife in the outback.

---

\* Langloh Parker, *More Australian Legendary Tales* (London: David Nutt, 1898), xv.
† Parker, *More Australian Legendary Tales*, xii.
‡ Jane Singleton, *What Katie Did: How a white woman in remote Australia notated an Aboriginal language and legends in the 19th century* (2020).

*Synkrētic*

While there needs to be a thorough examination of each of the *Legends* Katie retold in her *Aboriginal Legendary Tales* (*Legends*) first published in 1896, and their successors, that is to be done by those with the authority, the cultural knowledges, and permissions to do so which I do not have. There needs to be a similar examination of her *The Euahlayi Tribe: A Study of Aboriginal Life in Australia* (*Study*) which was first published in 1905.

I shall not attempt to explain or interpret the content of the actual *Legends* she collected and published, or the *Study*, in any way or to comment myself on their content.

This is a story of a remarkable woman and how some of the descendants of those who lived on and around Bangate in northwestern New South Wales and others with Euahlayi heritage, think of Katie and her work. With interest, with distress or as useful? It covers much of what has been written about her and her publications and further and importantly, whether those with the appropriate knowledges believe the *Legends* should have been published at all, as their publication may have broken sacred or esoteric law with catastrophic effect. It also looks at the ambivalence of Katie's description of Aborigines[8] as my 'darkie fiends', versus her understanding that she had settled on 'their land'.

Bangate Station was big. 215,000 acres (87,000 hectares) that included 38 kilometres of river frontage to the Narran River, which is doubled by the loop it took within the property. Despite the current drought there was still some water in it when I visited in July 2018 and the year before. In Katie's day it had invaluable Mitchell Grass pasture and in a good season was an excellent run. It still can be when the season is right.

Katie collected the *Legends* from the Noongahburrahs living on Bangate and working for she and Langloh. (Later she widened her work to other tribes further afield.) She was painstaking in her research and tested and retested her understanding of their language, Euahlayi. Her versions of the *Legends* were first published in 1896 as *Australian Legendary Tales*.

The 19th and early 20th century comments on the *Legends* were often dismissive. The actual legends were described as fairy tales and even Andrew Lang, the well-known English folklorist cum anthropologist who was one of Katie's earliest supporters, described them as mostly 'Kinder Marchen': fairy tales, or, more specifically, children's fairy tales. 'Children will find here the Jungle Book, never before printed of black little boys and girls. And the grotesque names are just what children like'. Nevertheless, he wrote long introductions to *Aboriginal Legendary Tales* and *More Aboriginal Legendary Tales* and *The Euahlayi Tribe: A Study of Aboriginal Life in Australia*. Katie, however, put folklore before children's tales. 'I have written my little book in the interests of folklore. I hope it will gain the attention of, and have some interest for children, Australian Children' (K. Langloh Parker, 1978).

Judith Johnston argues

that, while Katherine Langloh Parker gives way to pressure from the publisher and allows her work to go forward as designed primarily for the children's book market...the work had a far more scholarly focus. The very fact that her Preface first proposes her translation work as useful to the student and only subsequently of interest to children, indicates that for Parker this has been both an intellectual and a scientific process.[9]

An even more damaging put down than Lang's 'Kinder Marchen' was published in the widely read and prestigious *The Bulletin*. Critic A.G. Stephens wrote that the *Legends* have 'ethnologically little significance...seem to have been invented at a comparatively recent date'.[10] He suggested at the very worst that Katie may have confected them, and at the very least that the *Legends* were not ancient stories but recent and fed to a gullible white woman. Or that she was to be appeased as an inquisitor, however well-meaning, who held a position of power as employer, was white, and of the invader race.

Stephens dismissed her informants' culture as well as Katie's work, writing that 'the Noongahburrahs are evidently as happy in their thoughtlessness as all their kindred. The undoubted value of the collection is chiefly that of a literary curiosity ...the prattlings of our Australia's children, which even in their worthlessness must have charm for a parent'.[11]

*Synkrētic*

Katie firmly refuted this, writing: 'A dark skin is certainly a mask to most people, and so those who have it are little known.' She continued:

> I can safely say that every idea in the *Legends* in my books is the idea of a real Black—I am very careful to get them as truly as I can. First I get an old, old Black to tell it in his own language (he probably has little English) I get a young one to tell it back to him in his language; he corrects what is wrong, then I get the other one to tell it to me in English. I write it down, read it, and tell it back again to the old fellow with the help of the medium, or though I have a fair grasp of their language, I would not, in a thing like this, trust to my knowledge entirely…[12]

John Strehlow, the grandson of Carl Strehlow and Frieda Keysser who were contemporaries of Katie's,[13] more generously wrote of her work that 'while Western thought was trying to push Australian Aborigines down the scale of humanity, Lang and Parker were pushing them up.'[14]

Although Lang's fairy tale descriptor can now be seen as rather belittling of the *Legends* and of Katie's work, it is true that fairy tales were a highly regarded literary mode in the 19th and early 20th centuries. Lang, a leader of the folklore movement and well connected to her first publisher, David Nutt, most likely helped her get the early books published.

Lang was much more generous in his comments about her *The Euahlayi Tribe* published in 1905 than about the *Legends*. 'Mrs Parker's new volume, I hope, will prove that she is a close scientific observer, who must be reckoned with by students. She has not scurried through the region occupied by her tribe, but has had them constantly under her eyes for a number of years'.[15] 'Mrs Parker's book,' he continues, 'appears to deserve a welcome from the few who care to study the ways of early men, "the pit whence we were dug". The Euahlayi are a sympathetic people, and have found a sympathetic chronicler.'

In correspondence three years after he provided the introductions he says, 'It seems to me, from the account, that Mrs Langloh Parker's method of acquiring information is [as] good as it can be'.[16]

Much of this correspondence centred on the nature of Baiame, the overarching spirit or god she described and whether Baiame was a response to Christian influence or one purely pre-Christian or traditional, as she contended. Baiame, she argued, 'was a worshipful being revealed in the mysteries, long before missionaries came, as my informants aver.'[17]

'Certainly, she writes elsewhere, 'I have been fortunate enough in my experience of Blacks to have had to do with those free from mission taint.'[18] In the introduction to her *Study*, she writes that the 'nearest missionary settlement was founded after we settled among the Euahlayi and was distant about one hundred miles (160 kilometres) at Brewarrina. None of my native informants had been at any time, to my knowledge, under the influence of missionaries.'[19]

No armchair expert herself, she was very critical of the species. She wrote with acerbity about ethnography and anthropology and their practitioners of the time.

> I dare say little with an air of finality about black people; I have lived too much with them for that. To be positive, you should never spend more than six months in their neighbourhood; in fact, if you want to keep your anthropological ideas quite firm, it is safe to let the blacks remain in inland Australia, while you stay a few thousand miles away. Otherwise, your preconceived notions are almost sure to totter to their foundations; and nothing is more annoying than to have elaborately built-up, delightfully logical theories, played ninepins with by an old grey-beard of a black, who apparently objects to his beliefs being classified, docketed, and pigeon-holed, until he has had his say.[20]

Katie's work was at the forefront of one of the key anthropological discussions between two of the best known 'scientific' anthropologists, A.R. Radcliffe-Brown and A.P. Elkin. She also engaged with the writings of Howitt, Spencer, Muller, Mathews, Henderson, N.W. Thomas and, in respect of religion, Ridley, Tylor, Gribble and more. Anthropologist A.R. Radcliffe-Brown, working later than Katie and 30 years younger, did venture to Bangate, and in a letter to the editor of *American Anthropologist* discusses her and Adolphus Elkin's work. His trip is undated, but the letter appeared in the 1954 edition of that journal. He determined to compare Katie

*Synkrētic*

Langloh Parker, whom he said implied the existence of matrilineal local groups in her *Study* in 1905, with Elkin's and his own theories.

He rather ill-temperedly writes '…when I was investigating these tribes I made *a long and tiresome journey* to the Station where Mrs Parker had lived and was fortunate enough to find still there one of her chief informants, Helen and some other old members of the tribe…having spoken with Helen who remembered her [Katie] and others I have satisfied myself by the most careful enquiries from these persons that the local groups of Yualarai [Euahlayi/Yuwaalaraay] were patrilineal…I am quite certain of the accuracy of my account of these tribes in spite of Elkin's doubts'.[21]

With not a hint of Radcliffe-Brown's churlishness, anthropologist R.H. Mathews wrote in *Science of Man* in 1898 that 'I cannot conclude this article without expressing my appreciation of the labours of Mrs K Langloh Parker…she deserves the thanks of all who are interested in the folklore of the Australian Aborigines.'[22]

Finally, it is worth comparing Katie's method with Mathews' description of another self-taught anthropologist collecting stories a little after Parker. Whereas the latter extracted his information with 'long and patient hammering',[23] Katie's method involved patient listening and telling, listening and retelling, again and again, until the genuine narrative was found and agreed upon.

## Notes

1. *Daen*: An early transcription of the Yuwaalaraay word *dhayn* that refers to an Aboriginal man or person.
2. *Mopoke*: The southern or Australian boobook (*Ninox boobook*) is a common owl known as a "mopoke" in Australia.
3. *Nulla* (from *nulla-nulla*, also waddy, and boondi): An Aboriginal Australian hardwood club or hunting stick.
4. *Neilahman* (from *yiilaman*, also hielaman): An Australian Aboriginal shield made out of bark or wood.
5. *Dardurr*: A humpy or temporary shelter made using tree branches and leaves, bark, or grass.

6   *The Meamei*: A local Dreaming story of the Seven Sisters, the stars known in Greek mythology as the Pleiades.

7   *Euahlayi* has a number of English spellings. "Euahlayi" is the spelling used by Katie Langloh Parker and the spelling used by Jane Singleton in *What Katie Did*. "Yuwaalaraay" and "Yuwaalaraay" are now also used commonly.

8   In Jane Singleton's *What Katie Did*, Aboriginal people of the region are described as "Aborigines" when that is how they were described in the original texts.

9   Judith Johnston, 'The Genesis and Commodification of Katie Langloh Parker's *Australian Legendary Tales* 1896', in *Association for Study of Australian Literature*, Issue 4 (2005): 159-172.

10  Alfred George Stephens, 'The Red Page', in *The Bulletin*, No. 17, 9 January 1897.

11  Stephens, 'The Red Page', 1897.

12  Katie Langloh Parker, *My bush book* (Adelaide: Rigby, 1982); and Katie Parker and Andrew Lang, 'Australian Religion', in *Folklore*, Vol. 10, Issue 4 (1899): 489-495.

13  Belinda McKay, 'Writing from the Contact Zone: Fiction by Early Queensland Women', in *Hecate*, Vol. 30, Issue 2 (2004): 53-70.

14  Erica Kaye Izett, 'Breaking new ground: early Australian ethnography in colonial women's writing', PhD thesis, University of Western Australia, 2015, 333.

15  Katie Langloh Parker, *The Euahlayi tribe: a study of Aboriginal life in Australia* (London: Archibald Constable, 1905), x.

16  Parker and Lang, 'Australian Religion', 489-495.

17  Parker, *The Euahlayi tribe*, 5.

18  Parker, *My bush book*, 172.

19  Parker, *The Euahlayi tribe*, 2.

20  Parker, *The Euahlayi tribe*, 141.

21  A.R. Radcliffe-Brown, 'Letter', in *Anthropological Society of Washington*, Vol. 56 (1954).

22  R.H. Mathews, 'Folklore of the Australian Aborigines', in *Science of Man*, Vol. 1, Issue 71 (1898): 69-70; 91-93; 117-19; 142-43.

23  Mathews, 'Folklore of the Australian Aborigines'.

# The soldier who teleported from Manila to Mexico*

*Luis González Obregón*†

TRANSLATED BY *Zach Lindsey*‡

I

Restrain your terror, reader, for we're not talking about a spirit from another world, but rather a mysterious person who appeared one morning in the central plaza of Mexico City back in the 16th century.

The apparition certainly came from another world, but with its own flesh and blood; he travelled comfortably and without fatigue, and in less time than it has taken this pen to write these opening lines—though not by his own will.

We have found this little-known event in certain ancient parchments. It is verified by very serious authors, known for their veracity and theology. But let us get on with the story…that is to say, with the history.

---

* Luis González Obregón, 'Un Aparecido [An Apparition]', in Chapter 19, *México Viejo: 1521-1821. Noticias Históricas, Tradiciones, Leyendas y Costumbres* (Paris: Librería de la Viuda de C. Bouret, 1900), 181-185. This work is in the public domain.
† Luis González Obregón (1865-1938) was a Mexican writer. He wrote for *El Nacional*, was a member of the Mexican Academy of Language, and director of the Mexican Academy of History. He lived in Mexico City, Mexico.
‡ Zach Lindsey is a copy editor for the Institute of Maya Studies and holds an MA in Anthropology from Texas State University. He lives in Felipe Carrillo Puerto, Mexico.

# The soldier who teleported

In his book *Events in the Philippine Islands*, the prosecuting attorney for the appellate court in New Spain and consultant for the Holy Office of the Inquisition Dr Antonio de Morga[1] notes that, in Mexico, they first learned of the death of the governor-general of the Philippines Gómez Pérez Dasmariñas[2] the same day that he died. However, he doesn't discuss how or why they knew.

Certainly, in that day and age, when submarine cables had not even been dreamt of, it was surprising that on the same date on which an event happened, it was known from a distance as great as that separating Mexico from the Philippines.

This event, to which Dr Morga alludes in such a superficial and mysterious way, is narrated by others in more detail, although they attribute it to supernatural causes.

They say that, on the morning of 25 October 1593, a soldier in the uniform of those who lived in the Philippines appeared in the central plaza in Mexico City, and that this soldier, with rifle shouldered, asked everyone who passed by that place the usual and ritual, 'Who goes there?'

The chroniclers add that, the night before, he was standing sentry in a gateway of the wall which defends the city of Manila. Without realising it, and in the wink of an eye, he found himself transported to the capital of New Spain. There the case was considered so exceptional and stupendous that the Holy Tribunal of the Inquisition involved itself in the matter. After serious inquiries and the full legal process, it condemned the soldier, who had appeared so miraculously, to return to Manila. This time, though, he had to go the slow way, through Acapulco. This time, the road was longer. The spirit of Lucifer, who had caused the soldier's unexpected and sudden arrival, was to have no hand in the soldier's return.

## II

The events that we have described are recorded in thick parchments written by revered chroniclers of the orders of San Agustin and Santo Domingo. The details of the death of Gómez Pérez Dasmariñas described by one of these writers are particularly interesting to us.

Of all the nations that engaged most frequently in trade with the Spaniards in the Philippines was Japan, which was appreciated not just for its culture and politics, but for its well-designed cloth and other rich trade goods.

As governor of the Philippines, Gómez Pérez received an ambassador from the Emperor Taycosoma.[3]

'Around this time,' says Friar Gaspar de San Agustín, 'two ambassadors returned to Manila after a meeting with the king of Cambodia. One was Portuguese, named Diego Belloso, and the other Castilian, named Antonio Barrientos. They brought two beautiful elephants as gifts for the governor; these were the first ever in Manila. The purpose of this embassy came down to asking the governor for friendship, alliance, and aid against the king of Siam, his neighbour, who was trying to invade them. Governor Gómez Pérez Dasmariñas received the ambassadors warmly, and appreciated the gift. Not having enough manpower to offer the kind of help that the king wanted, he dispatched the ambassadors to give the king of Cambodia hope and, repaying him with another gift, established a good trade relationship between the two nations.'[4]

However, Dasmariñas realised this was an opportunity to conquer the Maluku Islands. To this effect, he sent an explorer, Brother Gaspar Gómez of the Society of Jesus, and acquired copious information from a second, one P. Antonio Marta who lived in Tidore.

Determined to achieve his goal, he acquired four galleys and a number of other vessels with a good number of soldiers, and on the pretext of helping the king of Cambodia they left Manila on 17 October 1593. They were accompanied by notable people and important religious figures.

The armada set sail from Puerto de Cavite on the 19th of the same month and year. On the 25th, however, an easterly wind forced the galley Capitana to abandon the others in the Punta de Santiago. This in turn forced Gómez Pérez to anchor in the Punta de Azufre. As the current was fierce, he had ordered the Chinese[5] he had brought with him to row harder. But there were 250 Chinese, and they were angered from being reprimanded with such ferocity by the governor. They resolved to rob the galley and all its supplies, and to do so they would have to kill all the Spaniards. This was easy because the rebels were many and armed.

Their scheme hatched, that very afternoon the Chinese all dressed in white tunics to be able to identify each other, and after having slit the Spaniards' throats, they waited until Gómez Pérez Dasmariñas was leaving his cabin and they split his head in two. His body, along with the others, was thrown into the sea, and, in such a devious way, the criminals got what they wanted.[6]

### III

There is no lack of chroniclers, as sensitive as they are harsh, who say that his death was punishment from Heaven. And it's true that, in his life, Governor Pérez Dasmariñas did not exactly agree with the Bishop of Manila, Friar Domingo de Salazar. They repeatedly argued about the affairs of church and state.

Take from that what you will, but the chroniclers note that in both Manila and Mexico, supernatural signs announced the death of the governor.

In Manila, for example, there was a fresco of Gómez Pérez among the portraits of the knights of the various military orders in the entrance hall of the monastery of San Agustín. On the same day he died, the wall on which the portrait was painted cracked, dividing the head of the governor in the same way his actual skull had been cleaved in two by his assassins.

'It's worth pausing to note,' concludes Friar Gaspar de San Agustín, 'that the same day of the tragedy of Gómez Pérez, they knew about it in Mexico through Satanic arts. A group of women who were inclined to such practices transported a soldier who was working at a sentry post on the wall of Manila to the Central Plaza [Zócalo] of Mexico City. It was done without the soldier feeling a thing, and the next day he was found wandering around with his weapons in the plaza. He was asking everyone around him who they

*Synkrētic*

were. But the Holy Office of the Inquisition of that city ordered him to return to the Philippines. There, he met many people who later assured me of the certainty of this event…'

When confronted with such an assertion by such a wise and prudent source, we should defer to the authorities and resign ourselves to repeating:

> If you the reader don't believe me,
> I'm just telling you what I heard.[7]

*Commentary*

This story tells of a strange occurrence reported to have happened in the Spanish colonial era. It may represent an attempt to rationalise the deep relationship between Mexico and the Philippines despite their geographical remoteness from each other. While Mexico is on the periphery of the Indo-Pacific, this story highlights the dense historical, political, and intellectual threads by which it is woven into the cultural fabric of the region.

The story is true in the sense that its author, González Obregón, may have heard or read it first-hand as he says. He does not appear to have overly embellished it. González Obregón has done a lot of the work for the reader to help them understand the history of the transported soldier story. He quotes Gaspar de San Agustín, an important historian and member of the clergy in Manila. San Agustín, who wrote the earliest-known version of the transported soldier story, notes that he was in the Philippines when he first heard it.

Another mention of the story, this one just ten years before González Obregón's Mexican version, appeared in José Rizal's footnotes to his 1890 edition of Antonio de Morga's 1609 *Events in the Philippine Isles*. We can surmise on this basis that the story probably came from the Philippines and moved to Mexico. But establishing when and how is more difficult.

Many questions surround Gaspar de San Agustín's 17th century story. The soldier "teleported" in 1593 but San Agustín did not write his famous work until 1698, more than a century after the supposed event. He reportedly did not leave for the Philippines until 1667, which puts more than half a century between the event and his arrival in Manila. San Agustín admits to having heard the story indirectly from 'many people'.

It may be that a Spanish soldier first told this story to folks there for the fun of it, perhaps to children, and that it caught on. Many Spanish soldiers in the Philippines came from Mexico, and any that came from Spain had to stop in Mexico on the way. 'Far from the image of adventuring, fortune-seeking professional soldiers of pure Spanish ethnicity,' as Stephanie J. Mawson writes, 'the companies of soldiers stationed across the Pacific consisted of half-starved, under-clothed and unpaid recruits, many of whom were in fact convicts, and were more likely to be Mexican mestizos than pureblood Spaniards.'[8] The average Spanish soldier would therefore likely have been able to describe Mexico City.

Still, even if a soldier had in fact been transported to Mexico City and forced to come back to Manila, he was likely long-dead by San Agustín's time. If he had been twenty at the time of his transportation, he would have been ninety-four by the time San Agustín arrived in Manila.

It would cast light on this mystery if an earlier version of the story were found. But the death of the governor of the Philippines was an important event, and the violence of it shocked people as far away as Mexico City. It is therefore no surprise that the governor's death does appear in earlier sources. A letter from the Viceroy of New Spain to the royal court in Spain detailed below does mention the governor's death and its fallout, for example, though not the supernatural events.

In his 1609 work *The Discovery and Conquest of the Molucco and Philippine Islands*, Bartholomew Leonardo de Argensola describes Governor Dasmariñas as a 'person of high reputation', but he notes that opinions on the governor were conflicted.[9] Given his claim that 'the Devil had possess'd' the Chinese sailors,[10] de Argensola would presumably have mentioned the stories of the transported soldier

*Synkrētic*

and the fractured painting if he had been aware of them. But he does not.

The timeline described by de Argensola also raises another problem for the interpretation of the story. In his account, it appears unlikely that the death of the governor was even known in *Manila* the day it happened. Thus, a soldier on sentry duty in Manila who teleported to Mexico City that evening would not have been able to take that information with him.

González Obregón's version of the narrative translated above implies that the speed at which the news travelled shocked one "Dr. Morga". Antonio de Morga is an important source because his 1609 *Events in the Philippine Isles* describes the governor's death and its fallout in detail. de Morga was in Mexico City around the time of the death.

But de Morga's actual comments are less dramatic than González Obregón implies. He proposes that the people of New Spain first suspected the death because they noticed a delay in the ships coming from the Philippines. This would make sense, as the governor's death coincided with a one-year hiatus in mercantile traffic until early 1594 due to storms.[11] But even this development must have taken some time to notice as only two or three ships a year usually embarked on the journey across the Pacific. Later in his work, de Morga mentions that, when he arrived in Mexico in 1594, its people still did not know about the governor's death.

Unfortunately for those fond of a good mystery, de Morga doesn't mention teleporting soldiers at all, nor do Argensola or the viceroy. It would therefore appear that the details of the myth were not cemented until many years after the governor's death.

In 1890, the famous Filipino thinker and polymath José Rizal translated de Morga's work into contemporary Spanish for a Filipino audience. He added a footnote to the passage about the way in which people in Mexico City learned of the governor's death: 'Remember the story of the soldier transported by witches to the Plaza in Mexico City—de Morga says he can't know how the news arrived.'[12] While de Morga does say this, he also suggests the much more mundane explanation of shipping delays.[13]

In any case, this footnote could imply that the story of the transported soldier was well-known in the Philippines by the 1890s, as Rizal asks us to remember a story which we are assumed to have heard before. But besides the work by Gaspar de San Agustín mentioned in the translation above, earlier iterations of the story are difficult to source in any Spanish-language book.

What was only a skeletal narrative in the late 1600s gradually grew skin and muscle over the centuries. At an unknown time, and much like its protagonist, the myth crossed the ocean from Manila to Mexico City. When it arrived, whether around the time that San Agustín's book, printed in Madrid, finally reached Mexico or later, the story confirmed what many people had heard: strange things had been afoot in Mexico after the governor died. Even if people in both places told the story in preceding centuries, it seems to have started blossoming in the 1800s.

There appears in Washington Irving's *Tales of the Alhambra* a similar short story dated 1832, 'Governor Manco and the Soldier', about a Spanish soldier who dashes from Castilla to the Alhambra in Spain.[14] In this story, the soldier is the one asked 'Who goes there?' when he arrives.[15] Both stories may play on tropes popular among the Spanish, including in this region which Irving had visited. But this story lacks the witches of the Manila-to-Mexico legend, the distance is much smaller, and the transported soldier is no messenger of death. The American writer Thomas Janvier suggested that, other than their remote ancestor in Arabian magic carpet stories, they were unrelated.[16]

By the late 1800s and early 1900s, the transported soldier story had become popular in the Spanish-speaking world and beyond. Shortly after González Obregón's Mexican version in 1900, an English version of the story by Thomas Janvier appeared in *Harper's Magazine*. Janvier claimed that the story was 'current across all classes of the population of the City of Mexico.'[17]

While Janvier mentions the González Obregón version, and his version begins similarly, certain aspects of the soldier's personality seem to have been taken from Irving. This could mean that the Janvier version was an amalgam of the González Obregón story and the previously unrelated Irving story, rather than a story he had heard from 'all classes' in the street of Mexico City.

In 1910, two years after publishing in *Harper's*, Janvier noted the similarities between his and Irving's stories but argued that they were unconnected. 'The transportation by supernatural means of a living person from one part of the world to another,' he writes, 'is among the most widely distributed of folk-story motives.'[18]

The major difference between the Irving story and the 1593 transported soldier narrative, according to Janvier, is that the latter includes actual events which, while historical at the time of San Agustin's writing, were nonetheless real. Janvier claims that the issue became so important at the time that even the Viceroy of New Spain investigated it. No extant historical sources suggest that the viceroy took an interest in the alleged paranormal circumstances related to the governor's death.

New versions of the story appeared into the 1930s and 1940s. In 1964, an issue of the Mexican comic *Tradiciones y Leyendas de la Colonia* brought the story to new audiences.[19]

The comic strip's writer invented a backstory about Governor Dasmariñas and his brothers. Despite its frivolous tone and anti-Spanish bent, the comic follows Spanish tradition by explaining the soldier's teleportation as the consequence of the reprehensible behaviour of Dasmariñas. In this version of events, the governor raped a woman and murdered her husband in Mexico before arriving in the Philippines. As far as I know, there is no historical evidence for either claim.

The writers seemed uninterested in the Philippines, with most of the action involving Governor Dasmariñas taking place in Mexico. Despite the Mexican government having declared 1964 to be the "Year of Philippine-Mexican Friendship", like many Mexicans, the artist had probably never visited the country and therefore lacked a frame of reference.

In modern Mexico, variations of the story appear in Mexican tabloids and occasionally in well-respected publications including *México Desconocido*. It has also made its way into United States culture, where some accounts attribute the mystery to witchcraft,

Satanism, inter-dimensional warping, and aliens among other conspiracy theories.

The story takes on an altogether different meaning in light of the colonial and modern relationship between Mexico and the Philippines. Art does not exist in a vacuum. It encodes the social, cosmological, and political values of its creators and the culture in which they live.[20] The same is true of narrative, which is rarely devoid of the symbols of the culture from which it emerges. It is no accident, then, that the soldier teleported from the Philippines and not from somewhere else, and it is no accident that he ended up in Mexico City of all places.

In the Spanish colonial era, the distance between Mexico City and the Philippines was difficult to overcome. To transport goods between Manila and Acapulco on Mexico's Pacific coast, the Spaniards built Manila galleons, which were some of the largest trading ships then in existence, which regularly made the journey across the Pacific Ocean between 1565 and 1815. They also created strict laws about who could travel and when.

The Spanish crown encountered issues in ensuring the compliance of conquistadors in New Spain because of the distance between the colony and the metropole. Messages between Spain and Manila took a painstakingly long time to send—and were often filtered through Mexico.

This delay in news caused systemic issues for governance. Although Governor Dasmariñas died in October 1593, for example, the Viceroy of New Spain, Luis de Velasco y Castilla, wrote a letter to the crown in January 1594 which did not mention his death.[21] He first mentioned the death in a letter written in November 1594, a full year after it happened.[22]

A minor issue of succession to the post of governor was even resolved before the viceroy had been made aware of the governor's death. Had he wanted to influence this decision, he would have been completely powerless to do so.

As for strange happenings, the viceroy did not mention anything pertinent in his November 1594 letter, although some of its pages are now damaged and unreadable. Presumably, he learned of the

*Synkrētic*

death of Governor Dasmariñas sometime between January and November 1594, as ships from the Philippines took about six months to arrive.

Many members of the church saw the influence of the Satanic all over the Spanish colonies. Dennis Tedlock goes as far as calling people like 16th century Spanish bishop Diego de Landa 'possessed' by fantasies about devils.[23] Gaspar de San Agustín, too, mentions witches and warlocks frequently in his work about the Philippines.

The González Obregón story suggests that Dasmariñas was no friend to the bishop, and may have been trying to increase the state's influence over the church.

After Mexico gained independence from Spain in 1821, by which time generations separated new storytellers from the death of Dasmariñas, the meaning of the story had changed. In the early 1800s, Mexico sought to redefine its relationships with colonial-era trading partners. While some of these relationships fractured, one which deepened even as its form changed was that with the Philippines.

The Manila galleon system, which utilised Mexico to transport trade goods from Manila to Spain for two hundred and fifty years, ended shortly before Mexico won its independence. While Spain would have to secure its supply of goods from the Philippines through other ports, trade flows between Mexico and the Philippines remained steady.

Today, the historical depth of this relationship remains politically useful, with the Mexican government describing the Philippines as the 'ideal entry bridge for Mexico's products in Southeast Asia'.[24] The Philippines is currently Mexico's 19th most valuable trading partner, while Mexico is the Philippines' 14th largest export market, the largest of any American country after the U.S.[25]

But maintaining these relationships took a lot of work over two hundred years. Beyond the daily grind of processing customs permits, Mexicans and Filipinos had to develop deep cultural affinities and people-to-people links. As well as being connected by migration, language, and possibly fashion (the *guayabera* and the *barong tagalog* shirts may be related), Mexico and the Philippines had substantive intellectual exchanges about independence.

One early supporter of Mexican independence, Epigmenio González, spent time in a prison in Manila where he may have influenced the burgeoning Filipino independence movement. Even as Filipino captain Andrés Novales was helped by Mexicans in his one-day uprising and effort to crown himself emperor in 1823, the Filipino Ramón Fabié y de Jesús joined Mexico's own independence movement, for which he too was executed.

The story of the transported soldier allowed people in the Philippines to "know" the people of Mexico and vice-versa by creating fictional places where their differences seemed less profound. In colonial Spain, stories such as this one might have served to shrink the empire to a more manageable scale.

Everyday Mexicans who told the story in the 1800s and early 1900s understood how far away the Philippines was. But although they likely understood that they were connected by a shared past and common dreams, most Mexican people would still only have known about the Philippines through news stories, word of mouth, and popular legends like this one.

This may explain the enduring appeal of the story of the transported soldier who crossed such a vast distance in the space of a witch's spell. And just like that, through his appearance in Mexico, these trading partners from different worlds became instant neighbours.

The other stories in González Obregón's book mix indigenous American narratives and European ones, and many of these legends, including of people turning into animals, are distinctly Mesoamerican. 'An Apparition', with its references to old Spanish documents, seems to skew more toward the European side. The final line of the narrative likely references a European source, for example. But González Obregón's reminder that the story can be entertaining even if it's not exactly true, and yet his refusal to admit that it is not true, parallels Mesoamerican storytelling practices.[26]

Specifically, it reminds me of something my teacher of Yucatec Maya used to tell me after she would tell stories about ghosts or

*Synkrētic*

goblins. At the end, I would ask, 'Do you believe that?' She would shrug and answer with a question: 'Do you?'

What is important is not the truth of the teleporting soldier, but what it says about the history and interests of the people who tell it. That it continues to entertain all these years later does not hurt, either.

## Notes

1 Antonio de Morga Sánchez Garay (1559-1636) was a senior Spanish official and lawyer in the Philippines, New Spain, and Peru. The work cited is Antonio de Morga, *Sucesos de las Islas Filipinas* (México: Casa de Geronymo Balli, 1609).

2 Gómez Pérez Dasmariñas (1519-1593) was the Spanish governor-general of the colony of the Philippines (1590-1593).

3 *An ambassador*. This may refer to Toyotomi Hideyoshi (1537-1598) or to Harada Magoshichirō (1590-?), his retainer who corresponded with the Spanish governor on Hideyoshi's behalf. Hideyoshi was a samurai who led a campaign to unite Japan and became its leader. He then invaded Korea. He carried the title *taikō* and was regent of Emperor Go-Yōzei. Ubaldo Iaccarino, 'Merchants, Missionaries and Marauders', in *Crossroads*, Issue 10 (October 2014), 159.

4 Friar Gaspar de San Agustín, *Conquest of the Philippine Islands* (Madrid: Parte primera, 1698).

5 *The Chinese*: Probably refers to a mixture of majority-Chinese, Indian, and other Asian men.

6 Some accounts suggest that the Chinese rebels failed to reach China and were turned around to face execution in Manila. In that city, the 1593 rebellion led to Chinese people being segregated and placed under military observation. Richard Chu, *Chinese and Chinese Mestizos of Manila: Family, Identity, and Culture, 1860s-1930s* (Leiden: Brill, 2010), 58.

7 Possibly a reference to the final two lines of the poem 'The student of Salamanca' (*El estudiante de Salamanca*) by José de Espronceda. The translator Nicolás Barbosa López renders these lines as: 'And reader, if thou say it is not true / As they have told it now I tell you'. See López, *Pessoa Plural*, No. 10 (Fall 2016): 391, lines 1011-1012.

8 Stephanie J. Mawson, 'Convicts or Conquistadores? Spanish Soldiers in the Seventeenth-Century Pacific', in *Past & Present*, Vol. 232, Issue 1 (August 2016): 95.

9 Bartholomew Leonardo de Argensola, *The Discovery and Conquest of the Molucco and Philippine Islands*, transl. John Stevens (London: J. Knapton, A. Bell, D. Midwinter, W. Taylor, A. Collins, and J. Baker, 1708), 125.

10. de Argensola, *The Discovery and Conquest*, 139.
11. Junald Dawa Ango, 'The Cebu-Acapulco Galleon Trade', in *Philippine Quarterly of Culture and Society*, Vol. 38, No. 2 (June 2010): 154.
12. Antonio de Morga, annotated by José Rizal, *Sucesos de las Islas Filipinas* (Paris: Libreria de Garnier Hermanos, 1890), 36, footnote 1.
13. Antonio de Morga, annotated by José Rizal, *Sucesos de las Islas*, 36.
14. Washington Irving, 'Governor Manco and the Soldier', in *The Complete Works of Washington Irving*, Vol. 1 (Francfort on the Main: Sigismond Schmerber, 1835), 1254-1259.
15. Washington Irving, 'Governor Manco and the Soldier', 1254.
16. Thomas A. Janvier, *Legends of the City of Mexico* (New York: Harper & Brothers, 1910), 159.
17. Thomas A. Janvier, *Legend of the Living Spectre, Harper's Magazine* (December 1908).
18. Janvier, *Legends of the City of Mexico*, 159.
19. Pablo Zambrano-Silva (ed.), *Tradiciones y Leyendas de la Colonia*, Vol. 38 (March 1964), available at: <https://tuul.tv/es/cultura/un-aparecido-leyenda-plaza-mayor>.
20. Robert Layton, *The Anthropology of Art* (Cambridge: Cambridge University Press, 1991).
21. Luis de Velasco y Castilla, *Carta del virrey Luis de Velasco y Castilla* (Jan. 1594), digitised at *Pares*, ref. MEXICO, 22, N.125.
22. Luis de Velasco y Castilla, *Carta del virrey Luis de Velasco y Castilla*.
23. Dennis Tedlock, 'Torture in the Archives: Mayans Meet Europeans', in *American Anthropologist*, Vol. 95, No. 1 (March 1993): 147.
24. Embassy of Mexico in the Philippines, 'Trade with the Philippines', in *Relaciones Exteriores*, available at: <https://embamex.sre.gob.mx/filipinas/index.php/negocios-y-comercio/tradewiththephilippines>.
25. Embassy of Mexico in the Philippines, 'Trade with the Philippines'.
26. For example, see Allen F. Burns (transl.), *An Epoch of Miracles: Oral Literature of the Yucatec Maya* (Austin: University of Texas Press, 1983).

# NOTES

# Muhammad's dream in the desert*

*Karoline von Günderrode*†

TRANSLATED BY *Anna Ezekiel*‡

i
In the midday blaze
Where no cooling breeze
Refreshes the desert sand,
Where, hot, kissed only by the simoom,[1]
A grey crag greets the clouds,
There the Seer sinks down tiredly.

i
*Bei des Mittags Brand*
*Wo der Wüste Sand*
*Kein kühlend Lüftchen erlabet,*
*Wo heiß, vom Samum nur geküsset,*
*Ein grauer Fels die Wolken grüßet*
*Da sinket müd der Seher hin.*

---

\* This poem was originally published as 'Mahomets Traum in der Wüste' in Karoline von Günderrode's first collection of poetry, dialogues, and short stories *Poems and Fantasies*, which first appeared in 1804. See *Karoline von Günderrode: Gesammelte Werke. Band 1-3, Band 1* (Berlin: Goldschmidt-Gabrielli, 1920-1922), 75-79.

† Karoline von Günderrode (1780-1806), a.k.a. Tian, was a German Romantic poet. Her works incorporated German, Persian, Indian, and Arab philosophical motifs. She lived in Frankfurt am Main, Germany.

‡ Anna Ezekiel is a feminist historian of philosophy working on post-Kantian German philosophy, especially the work of Karoline von Günderrode. She holds a PhD in philosophy from McGill University and lives in Hong Kong.

## Muhammad's dream in the desert

ii
    *Vom trügenden Schein*
    *Will der Dinge Seyn*
    *Sein Geist, betrachtend hier, trennen.*
    *Der Zukunft Geist will er beschwören,*     10
    *Des eignen Herzens Stimme hören,*
    *Und folgen seiner Eingebung.*

iii
    *Hier flieht die Gottheit,*
    *Die der Wahn ihm leiht,*
    *Der eitle Schimmer verstiebet.*     15
    *Und ihn, auf den die Völker sehen,*
    *Den Siegespalmen nur umwehen,*
    *Umkreist der Sorgen dunkle Nacht.*

iv
    *Des Sehers Traum*
    *Durchflieget den Raum*     20
    *Und all' die künftigen Zeiten,*
    *Bald kostet er, in trunknem Wahne,*
    *Die Seligkeit gelung'ner Plane,*
    *Dann sieht er seinen Untergang,*

v
    *Entsetzen und Wuth,*     25
    *Mit wechselnder Fluth,*
    *Kämpfen im innersten Leben,*
    *Von Zweifeln, ruft er, nur umgeben!*
    *Verhauchet der Entschluß sein Leben!*
    *Eh' Reu ihn und Mißlingen straft.*     30

vi
    *Der Gottheit Macht,*
    *Zerreiße die Nacht*
    *Des Schicksals, vor meinen Blicken!*
    *Sie lasse mich die Zukunft sehen,*
    *Ob meine Fahnen siegreich wehen?*     35
    *ob mein Gesetz die Welt regiert?*

# Synkrētic

|     | |
|-----|---|
| ii  | His spirit, here contemplating,<br>Will separate the being of things<br>From deceptive appearance.<br>He will invoke the future's spirit,     10<br>Hear his own heart's voice,<br>And follow his inspiration. |
| iii | Here takes flight the divinity<br>That delusion lends him,<br>The vain shimmer scatters.     15<br>And he to whom the peoples look,<br>Fanned only by palms of victory,[2]<br>Is encircled by the dark night of tribulation. |
| iv  | The Seer's dream<br>Skims through space     20<br>And all future times;<br>Now, in drunken delusions, he tastes<br>The bliss of successful plans,<br>Then sees his downfall. |
| v   | Horror and fury     25<br>Struggle in alternating spate<br>In innermost life;<br>Surrounded, he cries, by doubt alone!<br>May resolve breathe out its life!<br>Before regret and failure punish it.     30 |
| vi  | The divinity's might<br>Rends the night<br>Of destiny, before my gaze!<br>It lets me see the future,<br>Do my flags wave, victorious?     35<br>Does my law rule the world? |

*Muhammad's dream in the desert*

vii
*Er sprichts; da bebt*
*Die Erde, es hebt*
*Die See sich auf zu den Wolken,*
*Flammen entlodern den Felsenklüften,* 40
*Die Luft, erfüllt von Schwefeldüften,*
*Läßt träg die müden Schwingen ruhn.*

viii
*Im wilden Tanz,*
*Umschlinget der Kranz*
*Der irren Sterne, die Himmel;* 45
*Das Meer erbraußt in seinen Gründen,*
*Und in der Erde tiefsten Schlünden*
*Streiten die Elemente sich.*

ix
*Und der Eintracht Band,*
*Das mächtig umwand* 50
*Die Kräfte, es schien gelöset.*
*Der Luft entsinkt der Wolken Schleier*
*Und aus dem Abgrund steigt das Feuer,*
*Und zehrt alles Ird'sche auf.*

x
*Mit trüberer Fluth* 55
*Steigt erst die Gluth,*
*Doch brennt sie stets sich reiner,*
*Bis hell ein Lichtmeer ihr entsteiget*
*Das lodernd zu den Sternen reichet*
*Und rein, und hell, und strahlend wallt.* 60

xi
*Der Seher erwacht*
*Wie aus Grabesnacht*
*Und staunend fühlt er sich leben,*
*Erwachet aus dem Tod der Schrecken,*
*Harr't zagend er, ob nun erwecken* 65
*Ein Gott der Wesen Kette wird.*

*Synkrētic*

        He speaks it; then the earth
        Quakes, the sea
        Sublimates into clouds,
vii   Flames blaze from rocky chasms,        40
        The air, filled with the smell of brimstone,
        Sluggishly lets the tired shaking rest.

        In wild dance,
        The corona entwines
viii  The errant stars, the heavens;          45
        The ocean roars in its foundations
        And in the earth's deepest gorges
        The elements dispute.

        And concord's bond,
        That mightily entwined                 50
ix    The forces, it seems undone.
        The clouds' veil sinks from the air
        And from the abyss the fire rises
        And consumes everything earthly.

        In turbid spate                         55
        The blaze rises,
        Yet it burns ever purer,
x     Till from it arises, bright, a sea of light
        That reaches, blazing, to the stars
        And seethes pure, and bright, and radiant.    60

        The Seer awakens
        As if from the grave's night
        And, amazed, feels that he lives.
xi    Awoken from death's horrors,
        He fearfully awaits whether a god      65
        Of the chain of being now awakens.

## Muhammad's dream in the desert

xii
*Von Sternen herab*
*Zum Seher hinab*
*Ertönt nun eine Stimme:*
*»Verkörpert hast du hier gesehen* 70
*Was allen Dingen wird geschehen*
*Die Weltgeschichte sahst du hier.*

xiii
*Es treibet die Kraft*
*Sie wirket und schafft,*
*In unaufhaltsamem Regen;* 75
*Was unrein ist das wird verzehret,*
*Das Reine nur, der Lichtstoff, währet*
*Und fließt dem ew'gen Urlicht zu.«*

xiv
*Jetzt sinket die Nacht*
*Und glänzend ertagt* 80
*Der Morgen in seiner Seele.*
*Nichts! ruft er, soll mich mehr bezwingen:*
*Daß Licht nur werde! sey mein Ringen,*
*Dann wird mein Thun unsterblich seyn.*

*Synkrētic*

|     | |
| --- | --- |
| xii | Down from the stars
Down to the Seer
A voice now resounds:
'You saw here embodied
What will befall all things
You saw here the history of the world. |

<br>

xii

Down from the stars
Down to the Seer
A voice now resounds:
'You saw here embodied         70
What will befall all things
You saw here the history of the world.

xiii

The force drives
It works and creates,
Stirring inexorably;            75
What is impure is consumed,
Only the pure, the light-material, endures
And flows to the eternal primal light.'

xiv

Now night sinks
And gleaming dawns              80
The morning in his soul.
Nothing more, he cries, shall vanquish me!
Only let there be light! May that be my struggle,
Then my deeds will be immortal.

*Commentary*

This poem was published in Günderrode's first collection of poetry, dialogues, and short stories *Poems and Fantasies*, which appeared in 1804. Unlike Günderrode's play *Muhammad, the Prophet of Mecca*, the poem does not follow Muhammad's life or use the Prophet as a stand-in for European political figures. Instead, the piece develops Romantic, Christian, and alchemical themes to create an image of a creative genius radically transforming the world.

The poem 'Muhammad's Dream in the Desert' has little to identify it with the Islamic prophet other than the name itself and, perhaps, its setting in the Arabian desert. At the time Günderrode was writing, the figure of Muhammad was often used as a stand-in for Napoleon or Luther to critique European society and politics, and Günderrode herself used Muhammad this way in her drama *Muhammad, the Prophet of Mecca*.[3] However, this usage is not evident, or at least not prominent, in 'Muhammad's Dream'. Instead, the poem integrates influences from early German Romanticism, late eighteenth-century chemistry, alchemy, Neo-Platonism, and Christianity to create a rich set of images describing the remaking of the world.[4]

The poem begins with a common Enlightenment trope of a hot and sluggish Asia in need of refreshment and revitalisation.[5] The Seer is 'tired' and 'sinks down' onto the sand of the Arabian desert. This initial setting seems to call for a regeneration of the torpid earth, but several verses intervene before Günderrode will show us the world remaking itself (beginning from the seventh verse). I will discuss that apocalyptic vision below. But first, what is going on in verses ii-vi, after the Prophet sinks onto the sand?

In verse ii, the Prophet begins to develop insight into the true nature of the universe: he 'Will separate the being of things / From deceptive appearance.' This search for 'true' knowledge—that is, knowledge of something beyond or behind the everyday world of our ordinary experiences—was a frequent theme in Günderrode's work. It is the focus of her poems 'The Adept' and 'The Wanderer's Descent' and a major theme in her play 'Immortalita'.[6]

Günderrode would have intended this claim to be understood in the context of philosophical discussions about knowledge. In the first place, it likely includes a reference to Kant's distinction between the 'phenomenal' world of 'appearances' (of individual objects and events), which we encounter in everyday life through our senses and minds, and the 'noumenal' world of actual 'being', which is how the world exists 'in itself', unfiltered by our senses and mental processes, and which we can never know. Günderrode is also mobilising imagery of the 'lifting of the veil of nature', which was a prominent trope at the time, including in early German Romanticism, *e.g.* in Novalis' *The Novices at Saïs*. On this Romantic

*Synkrētic*

view, mystical visions can provide glimpses of the world as it exists 'in itself'—that is, beyond our ability to grasp with our senses and comprehend rationally. However, the cost of such visions may be madness or death. In Günderrode's poem, we see the Prophet teetering on the brink of insanity as he experiences 'drunken delusions', vacillating between megalomaniac dreams of power and crushing despair.

Also in the second verse, Günderrode indicates that insight into the true nature of things is to be gained through 'contemplating'. Specifically, knowledge of the universe is to be obtained by *inward* contemplation, or contemplation of oneself: by listening to one's 'heart's voice' and following one's 'inspiration'. This focus on the subjective experience of the individual, including as a means of coming to know the world, is typical of early German Romanticism, as well as of the work of the theologian Friedrich Schleiermacher. Günderrode studied these thinkers and integrated various aspects of their thought in her work.

However, Günderrode rarely if ever borrowed ideas from other writers without significantly modifying them, and 'Muhammad's Dream in the Desert' is no exception. Unlike the doomed protagonists of Romantic and Enlightenment seekers of hidden truths, Günderrode's Prophet penetrates the 'vain shimmer' of appearances and learns what lies behind them. At this point, he experiences existence beyond space and time: he 'Skims through space / And all future times.' Since space and time are essential categories that characterise and give structure to all our experiences, this indicates that the Prophet has passed behind the 'veil of nature' to perceive the world 'in itself'.[7]

Once the Prophet had reached behind the veil of appearances, he attempts to see the future and, specifically, what will come of his own plans and efforts to implement his will. But rather than obtaining answers, his questioning initiates a vision of an apocalyptic conflagration of the earth and its remaking into a new form. The seventh verse introduces Günderrode's description of the destruction and remaking of the world. The Prophet watches as 'the earth / Quakes, the sea / Sublimates' and 'Flames blaze from rocky chasms.' The stars as well as the earth are set into violent motion and conflict, until the whole world is destroyed by fire, which 'consumes everything earthly.'[8]

In this part of the poem, Günderrode uses hermetic and alchemical imagery, blended with ideas from late eighteenth-century chemistry, to portray the remaking of the world. Rather than being annihilated, the world that is 'consumed' by fire is transformed into 'clouds' and then 'light'. The word Günderrode uses is 'sublimates': a weighted term in both chemical theory and German philosophy (the term became especially famous in the work of Hegel). The original German verb, *aufheben*, can also be translated as to cancel, override, dissolve, or elevate. The burning of the world transforms earthly substances into a pure blaze of light which, Günderrode implies, is a higher or more spiritual form of matter. In the penultimate verse, a mysterious 'voice' explains that this resulting pure light-material[9] will merge with the 'eternal primal light': a metaphor for the divine.[10]

Günderrode's adaptation of alchemical and Neo-Platonic ideas becomes clearer in verse xi. Awakening from his apocalyptic vision, the Prophet wonders 'whether a god / Of the chain of being now awakens.' The idea of the chain of being, or the Great Chain of Being, originated with the ancient Greeks, especially the Neo-Platonists, and in mediæval Europe developed into a concept of the universe as organised hierarchically with God at the top, followed in order by angels, human beings, animals, plants, and finally rocks and minerals at the bottom. Each of these levels could be further divided into hierarchically ranked categories, for example mammals were seen as higher in the category of animals than molluscs. In alchemy, the supposed connection of all beings in a continuous hierarchy, like links in a chain, was seen as justifying the idea that one kind of being could be transformed into another. In this poem, Günderrode's use of the language of sublimation, materials being consumed, and repeated sinking and rising movements suggests that she may be depicting this sort of transformative transition between levels in the hierarchy of being.

*Synkrētic*

Lastly, at two points towards the end of the poem Günderrode uses Christian terminology to connect the Prophet's activities to the creative force of the divine—that is, specifically to God's creative word. In the second-last line, the Prophet cries 'Only let there be light!' (in German, *Das Licht nur werde!*), referencing God's creation of the earth in Genesis 1:3 ('Let there be light'; in German, *Es werde Licht!*). Similarly, the seventh verse, which ushers in the vision of the remaking of the world, begins with the phrase, 'He speaks it' (in German, *Er sprichts*). In these places, Günderrode is deliberately identifying the Prophet's speech with the word of God, which forms a new world out of the void or, in the Prophet's case, out of the old world. Linking back to the second and third verses, in which the Prophet's 'spirit' and 'divinity' guide his inner contemplation, it seems that Günderrode is presenting the inspired individual as developing, through introspection and the resulting penetration of the veil of nature, the creative power of a God.

# Notes

1 *Simoom*: a word used in the Middle East and the Sahara to denote a strong, dusty wind.

2 *Palms of victory*: the palm branch is a symbol of victory in Mediterranean, including Christian and Islamic, cultures.

3 Ruth Christmann, *Zwischen Identitätsgewinn und Bewußtseinsverlust. Das philosophisch-literarische Werk der Karoline von Günderrode (1780-1806)* (Frankfurt: Lang, 2005), 212; Karoline von Günderrode, *Poetic Fragments*, ed. and transl. Anna C. Ezekiel (Albany, NY: SUNY Press, 2016), 18, 123f; Lucia Maria Licher, '"Du mußt Dich in eine entferntere Empfindung versetzen." Strategien interkultureller Annäherung im Werk Karoline von Günderrodes (1780-1806)', in *'Der weibliche multikulturelle Blick.' Ergebnisse eines Symposiums*, eds. Hannelore Scholz and Brita Baume (Berlin: Trafo Verlag, 1995), 21-35.

4 Christmann also suggests the influence of ideas from Hemsterhuis and Fichte on the poem, and Solbrig identifies a further influence from Herder. See Christmann, *Zwischen Identitätsgewinn und Bewußtseinsverlust*, 176; Ingeborg Solbrig, 'The Contemplative Muse: Caroline von Günderrode, Religious Works', in *Germanic Notes*, Vol. 18, No. 1-2 (1987): 18.

5  There are obvious colonialist overtones in the associated ideas that: (a) the heat of Asia and Africa made people torpid and, correspondingly, stupid, unhealthy, and lazy; and (b) Asia had fallen from a state of former glory as the torch of civilisation passed to Europe. For the use of this trope by Günderrode and Goethe, see K.F. Hilliard, 'Orient und Mythos: Karoline von Günderrode', in *Frauen: MitSprechen. MitSchreiben. Beiträge zur literatur- und sprachwissenschaflichen Frauenforschung*, eds. Marianne Henn and Britta Hufeisen (Stuttgart: Heinz, 1997), 244-255.

6  These three pieces will all be available in English translation with commentary in my volume on Günderrode's work, *Philosophical Fragments* (forthcoming with Oxford University Press).

7  *Cf.* Günderrode's prose poem 'An Apocalyptic Fragment', which also describes a vision of the reality that lies behind appearances and which involves a disruption to the normal experience of time.

8  Günderrode's play *Udohla* includes similar imagery of a violent and fiery apocalypse, after which the world can be remade. For discussion of the role of revolution and the apocalypse in revitalising the world, and its importance in Günderrode's philosophy, see Anna C. Ezekiel, 'Revolution and Revitalisation: Karoline von Günderrode's Political Philosophy and Its Metaphysical Foundations', in *British Journal of the History of Philosophy* (forthcoming 2022).

9  In the late 18th and early 19th centuries, 'light-material' or 'luminous matter' (*Lichtstoff*) was thought to be a substance that emitted light. Later, this theory was shown to be incorrect and 'luminous matter' is now understood to be an imaginary substance.

10  Or, perhaps, a secularisation of the divine as a physical element.

# An onion with a thousand roots*

*Georg Christoph Lichtenberg*[†]

TRANSLATED BY *Christian Romuss*[‡]

It is almost impossible to bear the torch of truth through a crowd without singeing someone's beard.

Man in his true form actually looks like an onion with many thousands of roots, the nerves alone are sensible in him, the rest serves to maintain these roots and to relocate them more easily. What we see is therefore merely the pot in which man (the nerves) has been planted.

The mouth speaks what the heart is *not* full of—I have found this to be true more often than its contrary.[1]

To cognise *external* objects is a contradiction; it is impossible for man to step outside of himself. Whenever we believe we are seeing objects we are merely seeing ourselves. Of nothing in the world can we actually cognise something except ourselves and the changes

---

[*] The *Sudelbücher* were a series of notebooks or commonplace books kept by Lichtenberg during his life and published incompletely after his death. They are an unsystematic collection of aphorisms, witticisms, observations, and journal entries, and were highly esteemed by the likes of Arthur Schopenhauer, Sigmund Freud, Leo Tolstoy and Qian Zhongshu. They are in the public domain and available at projekt-gutenberg.org.

[†] Georg Christoph Lichtenberg (1742-1799) was a German physicist and satirist. He is known for his *Sudelbücher*, research on electricity, and for proposing the standard paper size ratio such as A4. He lived in Göttingen, Germany.

[‡] Christian Romuss is a Brisbane-based translator. He is deputy editor of *Synkrētic*.

which occur within us. It is likewise impossible to *feel* for others, as people tend to say; we feel only for ourselves. This proposition sounds harsh, but it is not so if it is only understood correctly. One loves neither father, nor mother, nor wife, nor child, but the pleasant sensations which they make for us; something always flatters our pride and our self-love. There is no other possibility, and whoever denies this proposition mustn't understand it. But in this regard our language cannot be philosophical, as little as it can be Copernican when regarding the cosmos. I believe the higher spirit of man shines forth no more strongly than in his ability to detect even the deception which nature, as it were, means to perpetrate against him. Only the question remains: Who is in the right? He who believes he is being deceived or he who does not believe it? Indisputably he who believes he is not being deceived is in the right. But both parties do not believe they are being deceived. For the deception ceases as soon as I know I am being deceived. The invention of language precedes philosophy, and it is this which makes philosophy difficult, the more so when philosophy is to be made comprehensible to others who do not themselves do much thinking. Philosophy, when it speaks, is always compelled to speak the language of unphilosophy.

About the incidents of life men do not think as diversely as they speak.

The donkey seems to me to be a horse translated into Dutch.

Men generally believe much less readily in miracles than in traditions of miracles, and many a Turk, Jew, *etc.* who would in this moment let himself be struck dead for his traditions would have remained very cool-headed had he been present when the miracle itself occurred. For in the moment when the miracle occurs it has no other credit than what its own worth lends it; to explain it in physical terms is not yet freethinking, as little as it is blasphemy to deem it deception. In general, to deny a datum is in itself something innocent; doing so only becomes dangerous in the world insofar as

*Synkrētic*

one thereby contradicts others who maintain its undeniability. Many a matter which in itself is unimportant becomes important in that it is made the concern of eminent people whom one considers important without actually knowing why. Like clouds if they are to be deemed solid, miracles if they are to be deemed true must be seen at a distance.

## Note

1  'For the mouth speaks what the heart is full of'. Luke 6:45. NIV.

# The critique of language*

## *Fritz Mauthner*†

TRANSLATED BY *Christian Romuss*‡

'[S]keptical resignation, insight into the unknowability of the world of reality, is no mere negation, is our best knowledge; philosophy is epistemology, epistemology is critique of language; to critique language, however, is to work on the liberating thought that, with the words of their languages and with the expressions of their philosophies, men can never get beyond a figurative depiction of the world.'[1]

### Eternal truths

Schiller's beautiful sentences are not the only things called 'eternal truths' in the language of our school essays. In philosophy too, for millennia, axioms have been readily called eternal truths, and even the personification of truth itself is occasionally given the epithet *eternal*, *timeless*, although such epithets pertain to people least of all. Fervent is the thought which imagines the Christian God to be the *summa veritas*, expressed by Augustine in a sentence which recalls

---

\* The following extracts are entries from Fritz Mauthner's *Wörterbuch der Philosophie. Neue Beiträge zu einer Kritik der Sprache* (Munich: Georg Müller, 1910/11). This work, *Dictionary of Philosophy: New Contributions to a Critique of Language*, is in the public domain in the original German and available on archive.org. It remains untranslated into English.

† Fritz Mauthner (1849-1923) was a Bohemian Jewish journalist, writer and philosopher. His best-known works are *Contributions to a Critique of Language* (1901-2), *Dictionary of Philosophy* (1910-11) and *Atheism and its History in the West* (1920-23). He lived in Berlin, Freiburg, and Meersburg, Germany.

‡ Christian Romuss is a Brisbane-based translator. He is deputy editor of *Synkrētic*.

## Synkrētic

Schiller: '*Erit [igitur] veritas, etiamsi mundus intereat.*'[2] Descartes, Spinoza, Leibniz, Kant speak, more or less critically, of eternal truths. But even in our own day, when the concept of truth has been psychologically investigated and recognised as a relative concept, when pragmatism on one side and Nietzsche on the other have introduced into philosophy Goethe's simple idea—namely, that what is biologically useful is called true—the talk of eternal truths does not cease; the logicians in particular happily recite the logical tautology that the truth of a judgment has no relation to time, is supratemporal, therefore eternal.

We will yet learn that *truth* and *belief* are not at all so very different from each other as the common language of our scholars believes or deems true.[3] Now, whoever finds himself incapable of teaching that a belief has eternal duration, that it is not historically formed and reformed, ought also to refrain from speaking of eternal truths. Truth is nowhere in the world except in human heads, and there too it is nothing more than a particular attentiveness, an affirmation of judgments and prejudgments which, even without this attentiveness or affirmation, have been deemed true. This applies to the most banal of *eternal* truths ('offences must be punished') up to the highest principle of the new worldview ('energy is constant'). Truths are not in reality, are only in human heads (Descartes: '*Aeternae veritates nullam existentiam extra cogitationem nostram habent.*'[4]), are strictly speaking only in human language, which is formed and reformed from people to people, from generation to generation. Eternal truths can therefore as little exist as there exists somewhere an eternal language. Even the proposition of the conservation or constancy of energy will not (in this form) eternally endure; and I do not mean the form of its words, but the form of its concepts.

## God

### Part I

It is often said: 'If God did not exist, we would have to invent Him.'[5] Would have to? We should say: would do well to. For the highest moral reasons. For reasons of a morality which is derived from the dictates of the existing or invented God. We really did have to invent him. Not because we were supposed to, but rather because it was in accordance with the nature of men and their language. That we had to invent God therefore means: We invented him—necessarily. The sense of the famous sentence is therefore: Because God does not exist, men, in accordance with their nature, invented Him.

God, the God of our word-inventory, the one or only God of the Christian West, is not to be understood as the generic concept of those imagined beings which the heathens called gods. Those gods were conceived according to the image of man. (Feuerbach was not the first to express this parodical thought; I find it already expressed in the *Theory of the Gods* by K. Ph. Moritz: 'Human imagination could attribute to the gods themselves no higher formation than that of man.'[6]) So they were images at least, images produced by a rich, young, beautiful imagination. The one God, on the other hand, is a mere word, an effortfully constructed word, without an image to depict its content. All attempts to see this paternal God figuratively are heathen. Protestantism with its iconoclasm was merely consequent.

If, for the purpose of comparison, we want to place this abstruse concept of God alongside other concepts, then we encounter the difficulty of finding words of similar nonsensity and yet of similar historical power.

The philosophers' stone never existed and yet miraculous powers were attributed to it. But the philosophers' stone was not only an article of human faith, but also in other respects real, an article of human making, as when it was fabricated and sold by fraudsters.

I prefer to compare God with the concept of phlogiston in chemistry. For almost a hundred years, from the end of the 17$^{th}$ until the end of the 18$^{th}$ century, the theologians of chemistry and with them the world believed in this word, which was supposed to explain the combustion of bodies, therefore heat, therefore the origin of the most important earthly force. We know today that lead oxide is lead plus something else, $Pb + O$. Back then it was taught, contrary to appearances—for the greater weight of lead oxide had already been observed—that lead is leadchalk plus something else, that lead is leadchalk (lead oxide) + phlogiston. Something which had never existed in the world was supposed to be the cause of something which did exist. Just as phlogiston was thought into every metal, so God was thought into all events: through God's providence hazard becomes history, through God's righteousness vengeance against a criminal becomes punishment, through God's invocation a statement becomes an oath.

The infamous ontological proof of God's existence is but one instance of many; man's habit of using illusory concepts allows the existence of those concepts to be imagined at the same time. Oldenburg, in a letter to Spinoza (27 Sept. 1661), already stated this beautifully: 'Do you believe you can prove clearly and beyond doubt from your own definition of God that such an entity exists? I of course think that definitions contain only concepts of our heads and that's all; that, however, our heads conceive much which does not exist, and are extremely fruitful in the multiplication and augmentation of things once conceived: I therefore cannot see how I am supposed to get from my concept of God to God's existence.'[7]

The respectable endeavour of Deism to serve in its way humanity's need for rest and to avoid the *regressus in infinitum* led to the acknowledgment of a God with which free thought believed it could get along. God is the answer to the most beautiful and childish question, to the eternal Why and to the Why of the Why. God is therefore the ultimate cause. Except that the subject and the predicate of this judgment are alike anthropomorphisms. Admittedly, in the fetish-making popular imagination, too, the concept of God is an answer to the old childish question, but this old God is created according to the image of man. And Hume sought to prove the boldest doctrine, namely that the concept of cause is also a kind of personification of temporal succession. Alongside such ideas, I don't know what is left of the Deists' judgment that God is the ultimate cause.

# Notes

1 Mauthner, *Dictionary of Philosophy*, Vol. I, xi.
2 'Therefore Truth will still be, even though the world should cease to be.' St Augustine, *Soliloquies*, transl. Rose Elizabeth Cleveland (Boston: Little, Brown, and Company, 1910), 55.
3 In the Western philosophical tradition, the distinction between truth (*aletheia*) and opinion or belief (*doxa*) is conventionally traced back to the poem *On Nature* by the $5^{th}$ century BC Greek philosopher Parmenides.
4 '[E]ternal truths which have no existence outside our thought.' René Descartes, *Principles of Philosophy*, transl. Valentine Rodger Miller and Reese P. Miller (Dordrecht: Kluwer Academic Publishers, 1982), 21.
5 '*Si Dieu n'existait pas, il faudrait l'inventer*'. This famous quotation first appeared in Voltaire's 1768 *Epistle to the Author of the Book of the Three Impostors*. In a 1770 letter to Frederick the Great, he added: 'But all nature cries aloud that he does exist, that there *is* a supreme intelligence, an immense power, an admirable order, and everything teaches us our dependence on it.' In *Voltaire in His Letters*, transl. S.G. Tallentyre (New York: G.P. Putnam's Sons, 1919), 233.
6 Karl Philipp Moritz (1756-1793) was a German editor and essayist. The full title of the referenced work is: *Götterlehre, oder mythologische Dichtungen der Alten* (Berlin: Friedrich August Herbig). The quotation is from p. 22 of the third edition.
7 For the full letter see Letter III, Oldenburg to Spinoza, 27 September 1661, London, in *The Chief Works of Benedict de Spinoza, Vol. II, Correspondence*, transl. R.H.M. Elwes (London: G. Bell, 1883-4), 279-282.

# An encounter with Father Ferriols

*Preciosa de Joya*\*

It was on my very first visit to the philosophy department that I fortuitously met Fr. Ferriols. I was a sophomore and had just decided to switch from political science to a philosophy major. As I handed in my form to the secretary, Fr. Ferriols stood nearby and, being a curious fellow, he asked me who I was.

Surprised at being questioned point-blank, I fumbled for an answer and blurted out my name, which was unremarkable. I was certain that it could only lead to an awkward silence, marking the premature end of our conversation. But to my surprise, it evoked the memory of someone he knew back in college. He asked me if I was related to a certain Antonio de Joya who had become a 'big shot' in the advertising business. While my parents had mentioned the name, I knew nothing about my grand-uncle, and was amused to learn about a distant relative from a stranger. What intrigued me was that Fr. Ferriols distinctly remembered "Tony" as an *inglisero*, an English speaker, who could hardly utter a word in Filipino.

'Unlike you,' he said, 'your Filipino is much better.' I couldn't see why that mattered. Filipino was mainly the language we spoke at home, which I grew up with and spoke while playing with kids in the streets of our *barangay*. But this stranger was clearly trying to convey the value of my aptitude in this language. As though to dis-

---

\* Preciosa Regina Ang de Joya is Lecturer at the Singapore University of Social Sciences. She holds a PhD from the National University of Singapore and is a former Fellow at the Institute for Cultural Inquiry, Berlin. She lives in Singapore.

pel my doubts, he then looked at me straight through his thick-rimmed glasses and uttered *bagay ka rito*, 'you'll fit right in here', in a prophetic tone.

At the time, I didn't know that this unassuming professor in a pair of faded, folded jeans and slippers was an institution in Ateneo de Manila University. Fr. Ferriols, or *Padre* as his students called him, was himself a 'big shot,' though he would never have admitted it. He always made fun of the expression in class, giggling naughtily as he translated it literally as *malaking putok*, meaning a strong whiff of body odour.[1] For Ferriols, language was not just words and grammar rules; it was alive and occasionally tickled with a sense of humour. At times, it packed a heavy punch, as when Ferriols responded to an *inglisera* student who complained about him insisting on teaching philosophy in Filipino. The story goes that the feisty professor looked at the student sternly and shouted, *Puta'ng ina mo!*, 'Your mother's a whore!' One could just imagine that poor student in a state of shock. But they say that, soon after this outburst of profanity, Ferriols smiled at the student and said, 'See, did you not feel that a lot more?'[2]

In our university, Ferriols was our Socrates and so much more. He was a pivotal force in the Filipinisation movement in the Ateneo, and one of the first professors to challenge the American Jesuits' rule of only teaching in English.[3] While his decision to teach philosophy in Filipino was a clear expression of support for the student movements of the 1970s, Ferriols himself felt that his ideas were often oversimplified and reduced to a political stand against the Americans. In fact, his indefatigable commitment to philosophising in Filipino was neither a rejection of the foreign, nor a simple injunction that students know themselves and their cultural heritage. It was instead driven by his desire to teach people to be open to the gift of encounter. This resolve was obvious to all who witnessed Fr. Ferriols, struggling with Parkinson's disease, literally inch his way to the classroom until his retirement at age 89.

For an encounter to be possible, the choice of language was crucial. Ferriols believed that a Filipino who philosophises in English, or in any foreign language for that matter, 'divorces reflection from the ordinary person.'[4] In his *Introduction to Metaphysics*, he asks:

> If a person whose knowledge comes largely from books…attempts to philosophise in the language that is different from that spoken by jeepney[5] drivers, street-sweepers, or street food vendors—can it still be said that that person is moving within the ambit of truth…or a lie[?][6]

One can infer from Ferriols' stern warning that a person who gives precedence to a language that plays no part in the life of ordinary folk runs the risk of refusing the wisdom that dwells in their own vernacular. Using this language has the unique potential to 'bring us together with' other users (*makasalimuha ang iba*) who contribute to its growth. Turning away from this, Ferriols asserts, is a form of self-deception insofar as it denies the fullness of reality, preventing ordinary people from taking part in the creation of knowledge and ourselves from being touched by a living language.

This awareness of reality and being faithful to what was really happening was of great concern to Ferriols. This was in reaction to what he saw as the main obstacle to thinking, namely the habit of getting caught up in our definitions and constructed world of ideas. To free oneself from being 'stuck in a concept', Ferriols would always encourage his students to ask, *Meron ba?* 'Is it really there?' Ferriols coined the term *meron*, drawing it from the Filipino word *mayroon* ('to have'), which he used as a metaphysical construct for the richness of existence. This term has often been equated to 'being,' but Ferriols always insisted that *meron* was not a mere translation of a foreign concept but the reflection of Filipino experience, one emerging from our own vernacular:

> It is not an unusual thing. We see it in any language. Heidegger says that *Sein* always has that moment of yes and no, in any language. And I saw that, in all Filipino languages, there is a moment of a yes and a no. In Tagalog, *meron* and *wala*, in Bisaya, *naa* and *wala*, in Ilokano, *atda*, *awan*, in Bikolano, *mayo*, *igwa*, in Panggasinan, *agkapu* and *wala*. [In this last example], *wala* is *meron*, and *agkapu* is *wala*. That is why, when I was using *meron*, in my thinking, I was returning [it] to its primary root… The root is, look at what is really happening before it became a concept. And if you are locked in concepts, use *meron* to get yourself out of [them].[7]

155

*An encounter with Father Ferriols*

In my years of teaching, I witnessed *meron* being ironically reduced to a concept. Students, especially those looking for an easy way to pass their philosophy course, latched on to a definition that they could easily parrot back during their oral examination. It took time for some of them to realise that meron was not so much an idea conveying the richness of existence as a way of seeing, of being constantly disturbed and touched by reality.

I remember approaching Ferriols in my senior year to ask whether he would supervise my undergraduate thesis. I had a brilliant plan to study the works of the Russian writer Fyodor Dostoevsky. I was excited when he readily approved, saying that it was a good project which no undergraduate student had ever done before. But a few months later, after realising the amount of work it would entail, I came to see Ferriols again to say that I had changed my mind, and that I was withdrawing my proposal. *Pasensya na po*, I courteously said, which translated in the simplest way means 'I'm sorry'. I will never forget what Ferriols replied that day. He gently corrected me, saying, *Pareho tayo magpapasensya, hindi lang ako, ikaw rin*. Translated literally, these words would seem to suggest that both of us—not just him but I as well—would have to be sorry. It was not something one would usually hear or say, but it was precisely because of their strangeness that I found his words disturbing and cryptic. It struck me how easy it was to blurt out the word *pasensya* (*paciencia* in Spanish, 'patience' in English) when seeking forgiveness, without really being aware of the weight of one's words.

Until then, I had been oblivious to the fact that saying *pasensya po* really meant asking for patience from a person one wronged or, in my case, whose expectations I felt unable to meet. In seeking forgiveness, was I simply asking for patience? For Ferriols, I too would have to learn to endure my own failing and grant myself time—a share of the future, a possibility—to have the courage to one day fulfil what I was then unable to.

# Synkrētic

## Notes

1. *Malaking putok* is a literal translation of 'big shot', but *putok* is also a colloquial expression for an 'explosion' of bad smell, of body odour.
2. Jim Libiran, 'Anong Meron sa Wala', in *Kwento, Kwenta, Kwarenta* (A Conference Tribute to Fr. Ferriols, S.J.), Ateneo de Manila University, August 2009.
3. After reopening the Ateneo in August 1898, the Jesuits gradually changed the system of instruction from Spanish to English in the hope of maintaining the Ateneo's reputation as Manila's 'premier school'. In a world where English was becoming the *lingua franca*, it was believed that the use of Spanish in the classroom was only depriving Ateneo of 'a golden chance to be of real service to the people.' In 1921, the Philippine Mission was entrusted to the American Jesuits of the Maryland-New York Province, and Ateneo, as part of its Americanisation, became an English-speaking school. For more details, see Jose S. Arcilla, S.J., 'Ateneo de Manila: Problems and Policies, 1859-1939', *Philippine Studies*, Vol. 32, No. 4 (1984): 377-398.
4. Roque Ferriols, S.J., interview, 2009.
5. *Jeepneys*, initially made out of repurposed U.S. Army Jeeps, are a popular means of transportation in the Philippines.
6. Roque Ferriols, S.J., *Pambungad sa Metapisika* (Quezon City: Office of Research and Publications, Ateneo de Manila University, 1997), 236.
7. Ferriols, interview, 2009.

# Fr Roque J. Ferriols, SJ (1924-2021)*

## *Tony La Viña*†

The motto of Ateneo de Manila University in Latin is *Lux in Domino*, translated as 'Light in the Lord'. The phrase comes from the letter of St Paul to the Ephesians: 'For you were once darkness, but now you are light in the Lord. Live as children of light (for the fruit of the light consists in all goodness, righteousness and truth).'[1]

Fr Roque Ferriols SJ, whose mortal body left us on Sunday 15 August 2021,[2] the Feast of the Assumption, is truly light for generations of Ateneo de Manila students as well as all over the Philippines, since his students became teachers in many other schools. Padre Roque is light to Filipino philosophy and philosophising in Filipino. He is light not only to minds but also to hearts that desired the mercy of the Lord.

Padre Roque—who was only one day short of 97, 80 years a Jesuit, 67 years a priest, more than 50 years a philosophy teacher—is the most brilliant and wisest Filipino I have ever met. He ranks up there with Jose Rizal and another Jesuit, Fr Horacio de la Costa, in

---

\* This piece was first published by *Rappler* as 'Padre Roque, who helped us see the light', 18 August 2021, available at: <www.rappler.com/voices/thought-leaders/opinion-roque-ferriols-helped-us-see-light/>. It is reprinted with the gracious permission of *Rappler*'s editor. The article has been edited and some original content added to it.

† Antonio Gabriel M. La Viña teaches law and is former dean of the Ateneo de Manila University's School of Government. Professor La Viña holds an SJD from Yale University. He lives in Manila, the Philippines.

*Synkrētic*

his mastery of languages,³ depth of insight into our culture and what makes us Filipinos, and in the elegance of his writing. As his classmate Fr Catalino Arevalo SJ, also a towering Jesuit intellectual and theologian, said quoting Fr De La Costa: 'Roque Ferriols is the only true genius we have among the Philippine Jesuits.'⁴

Padre Roque taught me two philosophy courses: one on ancient and mediæval philosophy, and the other on Søren Kierkegaard. My biggest regret as an Ateneo de Manila philosophy major is that I was not able to take more courses with him. This was because, as a Cebuano-speaking *Bisdak* from Mindanao, I initially felt intimidated by the course requirement that we read and write in Filipino. It took me a while to conquer that fear, which I was eventually able to. In fact, a few years later I also started teaching philosophy in Filipino.

I have fond memories of my many encounters with Fr Roque, including of how he looked at me with a naughty grin one time in his ancient philosophy class after I asked a stupid question. 'With a question like that,' he responded, 'I should throw the eraser to you. Instead, I will just smile!' I remember, too, how he entered the classroom the day John Paul II was elected Pope, excited that a philosopher who knew phenomenology was now Pope. Or that time in 1985 when he learned that I had chosen Camiguin as my honeymoon destination. Roque said to Diane, the department secretary, that only I would choose that island, which at the time had no fancy hotels. I felt so proud, even if undeserving, to meet him again in 2004 on his 80th birthday after many years of being away in the U.S. He looked at me and said, 'You are the lawyer of the oppressed.' I supposed that he remembered our conversations when I was still a law student at the University of the Philippines while also teaching philosophy in Ateneo de Manila.

My mind and heart were forever changed by the experience of being in a Ferriols classroom. It confirmed the reason why so many of us who were non-seminarians chose or shifted to philosophy in college. In our forms, we used to write in response to the question 'Why shift to philosophy?' with 'I saw the light'.

Padre Roque helped us see the light. It was not just that he enabled us to go back to the time of the first Greek philosophers, the pre-Socratics, to share in their first experience of abstraction. It was not just that Padre Roque helped us put on the eyes and heart of a Socrates and an Augustine searching for the truth that matters. It was not just being given an insight into the agony—the fear and trembling—and faith of the Danish philosopher Kierkegaard. Above all, Padre Roque taught us how to think, how to ask questions, how to wonder, ultimately to search for God, which leads us to the discovery that it is God who searches for us. We will never forget Fr Ferriols' words, *Isa lang ang mahalaga sa buhay: hanapin ang kalooban ng Diyos at tupdin ito*, meaning: 'There is only one thing important in life: find the will of God and obey it.'[5]

Aside from the two courses he taught me and like many others, I was also a student of Padre Roque vicariously through his students, who became my teachers. These included Dr Ramon Reyes who was my mentor in modern and contemporary philosophy and made Hegel, Kant, and Husserl familiar to me; Dr Leovino Garcia who introduced me to Levinas and Ricœur and whose relationship with Padre Roque has always been edifying; Dr Manny Dy who was my ethics and Chinese philosophy teacher; Fr Joel Tabora SJ who was my mentor in understanding Karl Marx; Rayvi Sunico who taught us the philosophy of religion during our undergraduate years and Plato when we were graduate students; and Pablito Perez, now a Justice of the Court of Appeals who was my first philosophy teacher, who confirmed to me by his example of philosophising in the classroom that I was taking the right college major. Although I was never his student, Dr Eddie Calasanz should be on the list because of his immense intellectual and personal influence in my life.

My students in law, philosophy, and governance can also claim to have vicariously been taught by Padre Roque, as much of what I teach would be rooted in my own philosophical education. Certainly, my sons—all Ateneo alumni and two of whom were philosophy majors in college—were also taught in this way by Ferriols.

As his co-teacher, I was able to have many conversations with Padre Roque and learned even more from him. It was during those years that he also became more prolific in writing as he discovered the wonders of word processing and the personal computer. That allowed him to write many books, all in Filipino, in which he asked the most profound questions about being, which he translated as *meron* and explained as a dynamic reality or process of *pagmemeron*,[6] about being and becoming human or *pagpapakatao*, and always about God.

In his *Philosophy of Religion*,[7] he translates a text on hope by Gabriel Marcel and excerpts from Saint Augustine's *Confessions*, which he translates in a stroke of genius as *Pag-amin at Papuri*. I literally cry when I use these texts in my seminary classes because of the beauty of Marcel's and Augustine's ideas, which are made even more beautiful and accessible to the reader by Padre Roque's mastery of Filipino.

I cannot think of a better example of the teacher and writer that I wanted and want to be than Padre Roque. I cannot think of a better life, lived fully in wisdom and holiness than that of this priest and Jesuit. We see this in his book *Glimpses into my beginnings*, which is Ferriols' memoirs of his life as a young Jesuit during World War II when Manila was under Japanese occupation.[8]

In that book, Ferriols recalls the Battle of Manila and describes seeing the body of a dead Japanese soldier: 'I saw a dead Japanese soldier sprawled on the street, face up. I knew he was a Japanese soldier because of his shoes. Except for his pair of shoes, he was not wearing anything. He was completely naked, and his penis was erect. Someone threw some earth at his body. Oil had been dumped on his face. But you could make out the emotions he had before he died. His face was that of a young boy gripped by fear. The last thing he saw in his dying moments was what triggered his fear. And a voice told me, "Don't ever forget that these Japanese are human. Never forget this. All human beings are human."'

Even then, in 1945, three years before the United Nations General Assembly adopted and proclaimed the Universal Declaration of Human Rights, Fr Roque understood the meaning and the transcendental importance of human rights.

*Fr Roque J. Ferriols, SJ*

In the final chapter of this book, Padre Roque recalls a spiritual conference with Fr de la Costa, reflecting on what they had just gone through during the Japanese occupation and the Battle of Manila:

'He reminded us that we were facing the long discipline of studying to be a Jesuit. In all these undertakings, whatever your field may be, never forget, he reminded us, that Christ is in everything and he will always be with us. For in the beginning was the Word, and the Word was God, and without the Word, there will be no creation.[9] The Word became flesh...Christ is the Word.[10] He is with us in everything. Always. He will fill our nets with fish to the brim, if we wait patiently the whole night through...we will cast our nets though we catch nothing.[11] He will make our wine his blood,[12] when we are hardly able to walk as we come from the hell...the earthen jar overflowing with water precariously on our back.[13] He will feed the teeming multitudes whenever we share with them what little we have.'[14]

Fr Roque goes on to say: 'It is through our bread and two fish and a poem that we begin metaphysics.' In the same chapter, he also shares a beautiful poem which concludes with what he has always taught us, that 'the end is always the beginning.'

Padre Roque was Light in the Lord. For those of us who were blessed to have been taught by him, he helped us see the light. Padre helped us live as children of light. With God's grace and imperfect as we were, he enabled us to produce also some goodness, righteousness, and truth. We will always be grateful to him.

## Notes

1. Ephesians 5:8-9. NIV.
2. Paterno R. Esmaquel II, 'Father Roque Ferriols, pioneer of philosophy in Filipino, dies at 96', in *Rappler*, 15 August 2021, available at: <https://www.rappler.com/nation/jesuit-priest-father-roque-ferriols-dies-august-15-2021>.
3. Roque J. Ferriols, 'North Sampalokese is better than Plato's Greek', in *Synkrētic*, №1 (Feb. 2022): 103-106.
4. Also cited in Esmaquel II, 'Jesuit Roque Ferriols turns 90, touches lives of youth', in *Rappler*, 16 August 2014 available at: <https://r3.rappler.com/rappler-blogs/paterno-esmaquel/66423-jesuit-roque-ferriols-ateneo-youth>.
5. *Cf.* Ecclesiastes 12-13, NIV: 'Now all has been heard; here is the conclusion of the matter: Fear God and keep his commandments, for this is the duty of all mankind.'
6. Florentino T. Timbreza, 'Filipino logic', in *Synkrētic*, №1 (Feb. 2022): 107-110.
7. Roque Ferriols, *Pilosopiya ng relihiyon* (Quezon City: Bluebooks, 2014).
8. Roque Ferriols, *Glimpses into my beginnings* (Manila: Ateneo de Manila University, 2016).
9. John 1:1.
10. John 1:14.
11. Luke 5:1-11; John 21:1-14.
12. Matthew 26:28.
13. *Cf.* Luke 22:10.
14. Matthew 14:13-21; Matthew 15:32-39.

# The silence of Thai history

*Thongchai Winichakul\**

Professor Winichakul, you are a Thai historian. In your new book, *Moments of Silence*,[1] you draw on your experience in the 6 October 1976 massacre in Bangkok. Were you a student at the time?

Yes, a second-year student.

'We beg you, please stop shooting!' This is what you reportedly said to Thai police on the day of the Thammasat University massacre in 1976, which you witnessed. What happened on that day which is still surrounded by silence?

Thousands of people gathered at Thammasat campus to protest the return of a former dictator, which, we believed, was part of the plot for the return of military rule. All institutions of the establishment—military, police, media, and the palace—conspired to effect a brutal suppression with deadly force. Forty were killed in a few hours, thousands arrested. Many corpses were desecrated by hanging, burning, dragging their bodies around on the ground, and nailing sticks into their chest as if they were demons. A female corpse was sexually desecrated. The brutality and the desecrations that morning were beyond comprehension.

---

\* Thongchai Winichakul is Professor Emeritus of History at the University of Wisconsin-Madison. He earned his PhD from the University of Sydney and a BA from Thammasat University. He lives in Madison, Wisconsin, U.S.A.

I explain in my book the reasons for the silence of different parties involved in the tragedy. These reasons also changed depending on changing political contexts during the forty years since the massacre.

**In the book, you mention a friend of yours who was beaten and killed by police, whose autopsy you later found, confirming the fact and conditions of his death. From your research, are any other victims still unaccounted for?**

We don't know if there were more. Among the forty bodies, three males were unidentified and four burnt beyond recognition. There was no investigation whatsoever, right after the incident or until now. The Thai state wants its crimes to be forgotten. Some groups of people tried to find out about the victims. But without cooperation, it is very hard, probably impossible. And without regime change—from a royalist state to a democracy—a serious investigation is unlikely.

**After the Bangkok massacre, you came to study at the University of Sydney in the 1980s, where you earned your master's and doctoral degrees. What are your memories of your time in Sydney? Have you been back since?**

I was fortunate to get a scholarship from the University of Sydney in 1982. Sydney was my first experience outside Thailand. I didn't have opportunity to travel to learn much about vast Australia. My interest was elsewhere anyway. For me, reading and writing English was tough. It took tremendous efforts and time to adjust. Above all, my Sydney years were the time I looked back, to come to terms with the tragedy, to find the purpose, to move on without ever forgetting. For me, libraries, books, and time for introspection helped me to get through.

Luckily, I was able to write an alternative history of Thailand as a way to fight back against the cruel massacre.

Given my work in the U.S. Midwest for most of my career, it is very far to travel to Sydney. I went back only once in 2014. It was

## The silence of Thai history

quite a different city from the one I knew in the 1980s. But the apartment where I used to stay was still there and unchanged. I also visited the libraries where I spent most of the time during my life in Sydney.

**In 1988, you completed your PhD on the topic of the history of maps of Siam or Thailand. At the time, you wrote one essay introducing Orwell's *1984* to Thai readers, and another in 2008. Is the book popular in modern Thailand?**

Orwell's *1984* was not part of my study. It was a small part in the process to make sense of the horrible Thailand. But it is quite powerful for readers who live in a subtle authoritarian condition as in Thailand. The book was translated for the first time in 1982 (not by me) when democratisation in Thailand was under way. I don't think it was known beyond a small intellectual circle. The translation was reprinted in 2008 in a quite different environment, that is, in the repressive political and cultural conditions after the 2006 coup. Since then, *1984* has been read widely and is known, mostly by the younger generations. Reading the book in public has also become a form of protest that individuals can engage in at any time and in any place. I don't know how many times it has been reprinted.

**Does Thailand have a George Orwell, an essayist, philosopher, or other polemicist whom you could recommend to readers unfamiliar with Thai literature or who can't read Thai but would gladly pick up a translation?**

Intriguing question.

There are, of course, writers of many kinds including columnists. But I understand the meaning of an essayist and its difference from other kinds of writers, say a columnist. Only a few Thai writers, in my opinion, are thoughtful, sophisticated, and write beautiful essays that show the power of prose like an essayist does. I wonder if there is the essayist tradition in the Thai language, similar to the one in English.

*Synkrētic*

If there is none, the question is why? I don't think Thais are less sophisticated nor the Thai language less powerful than English. Perhaps it has to do with cultural conservativism that controls words and establishes the regime of proper expressions from childhood to higher education. Perhaps it has to do with the lack of freedom beyond the realm of proper politics but indeed in the tradition of writing, thus the under-appreciation and under-realisation of the power of prose. Perhaps it has to do with the supremacy of conservative Buddhism that stifles imagination, thinking outside the box, and thoughtfulness. I have never thought about this question.

**Thailand has a unique history as the only Southeast Asian country never colonised by Europeans. Does its intellectual history, philosophy or general culture reflect the idea of Thailand having a special historical mission?**

The misunderstood "unique history" has been the basis of the royalist historical ideology that can turn as cruel as it did in 1976. Thailand's history is unique in the sense that every history is particular, thus not unique in this sense. But its colonial history is far from unique if we look further afield to Persia, Turkey, and other semi-colonies, or if we take the "colonial" not merely as the direct rule by a foreign power, but a condition of subjugation—directly or otherwise, formally or not, varied in degrees and forms—by an imperial power. In the case of Siam, it was both semi-colonised and itself was an imperial power too. Its colonial relations with European powers, that is the West, on the one hand, and its subordinates on the other were the actual condition of Siam's peculiar modernity. The notion of "never colonised" is either naïve or ideological (a piece of propaganda) or a touristic history for easy consumption.

Its ideologically "unique history" is a crucial component of the protectionist, provincial mentality of Thailand, by which I mean the pride in its unique past, philosophy, and culture which nobody else could fully understand, and the sense of transcendental fulfilment despite (indeed because of) this provincialism. If there is a historical mission, it is to unlearn and unravel this supposedly unique history, and to recognise its semi-colonial and semi-imperial conditions. This is quite crucial to fighting the oppressive intellectual culture, to unlock the potential of history, philosophy, and general culture from the domination of the state's ideology and the state's Buddhism. To set free imagination.

**Britain had Herbert Butterfield's Whig view of history and E.H. Carr's famous *What is History?* (1961). Germany had Leopold von Ranke and Hegel. Is there a Thai tradition of historiography or philosophy of history?**

Thailand is not yet a "nation-state" in the classic sense. It is a modern royal-nation, not an archaic kingdom but an imagined national community of royal subjects. Its historiography is still predominantly royal-nationalistic. In my view, the philosophy of this history is simplistic and derivative, nothing original or interesting. It is quite powerful, nonetheless, perhaps thanks to its simplicity. Fortunately, alternative historiographies have begun to emerge in recent decades and gained traction.

**In a *New Mandala* interview,[2] you said that you have thought about the 1976 massacre every day for the past 40 years. The massacre's perpetrators were amnestied in the end. What would you like to see in order to feel a sense of justice?**

I hope one day there would be as thorough an investigation as there could be, even though it might be late. I hope that dignity would be restored to every death—to their names and their bodies—and to their families too. I hope the wrongdoing in all forms and the perpetrators at all levels would be spelled out in public. They deserve appropriate punishment no matter how late, and their names and honour repudiated no matter how majestic they were or are. No vengeance, but justice and morality must be restored. The disgusting impunity must end so the rule of law can begin.

If all this could be achieved before the end of my life, however, I am not sure how I would feel. I myself don't need such closure anymore in order to move on. Besides, it is already too late for me to appreciate the sense of justice, and not to feel how cruel history can be.

Memory work takes many forms, from truth commissions as in Rwanda and South Africa, to joint history textbooks as in Europe, to documentaries like *The Act of Killing* in Indonesia. Are such processes underway in Thailand?

As I write in the book, in recent years the silence surrounding the massacre has been broken. Information about the tragedy has gradually been openly and widely circulated. Despite that, limits to what can be said about the tragedy remain. The who and why remain unspeakable. These memory works are the result of intellectual works (articles, books, memoirs, *etc.*) and commemorative activities by the survivors over the past twenty years, and in the past few years by political activists of the younger generations. I would say the process has been underway by citizens who care. The memory movement remains small, but it is noisy and very loud, influencing the memories of other atrocities in this land. The state has remained in total silence as ever, as if the massacre never occurred.

## Notes

1 Thongchai Winichakul, *Moments of Silence: The Unforgetting of the October 6, 1976, Massacre in Bangkok* (Honolulu: University of Hawai'i Press, 2020).
2 See 'Thongchai Winichakul and his book on the Thamassat University massacre', in *New Mandala*, 2 November 2021, available at: <https://www.newmandala.org/nbseas-thongchai-winichakul-and-his-book-on-the-thamassat-university-massacre/>.

# Spurned by philosophers*

*Han Shan*†

TRANSLATED BY *Span Hanna*‡

## I. Living and dying

| | |
|---|---|
| 庄子说送终， | An old sage[1] said, when his time came to die |
| 天地为棺椁。 | to lay his coffin between the earth and sky. |
| 吾归此有时， | When this occasion comes around for me, |
| 唯须一幡箔。 | a reed mat on a pole is all I'll need. |
| 死将谓青蝇， | From my corpse the green flies will get a feed, |
| 吊不劳白鹤。 | the white crane easily sing a eulogy. |
| 饿著首阳山， | What's left, dump on a hillside in the sun. |
| 生廉死亦乐。 | Living and dying turn out to be just as much fun. |

---

\* These translations were first published as poems 15, 30, 277, and 292 in Han Shan, *Songs from Cold Mountain*, transl. Span Hanna (Norwood, South Australia: Moon Arrow Press, 2019), 38, 53, 315, 330.

† Han Shan (est. 720-810 CE), literally 'Cold Mountain', was a Chinese Buddhist poet and recluse. Whether he was a real person or Han Shan is merely a pen name is not known. He likely lived in Tiantai, Zhejiang Province, China.

‡ Span Hanna is an editor and Chinese language translator. He studied Chinese for a BA at the University of Adelaide and has taught and translated Chinese in primary school and other settings. He lives in Melbourne, Australia.

## II. Spurned by philosophers

| | |
|---|---|
| 智者君抛我， | By gentleman philosophers I'm spurned, |
| 愚者我抛君。 | and I, acting the fool, spurn them in turn. |
| 非愚亦非智， | Neither knowing nor a fool, indeed, |
| 从此继相闻。 | our mutual discourse can from here proceed. |
| 入夜歌明月， | The shining moon becomes the song of night, |
| 侵晨舞白云。 | dawn's approach the dance of clouds so white. |
| 焉能住口手， | Thus with the simplest needs do I get by, |
| 端坐鬓纷纷。 | crosslegged, wild hair waving at the sky. |

## III. On the wheel

| | |
|---|---|
| 自古诸哲人， | Of all the philosophers of ancient times, |
| 不见有长存。 | not one has ever attained longevity. |
| 生而还复死， | No sooner born than heading back to death, |
| 尽变作灰尘。 | becoming dust and ash their destiny. |
| 积骨如毗富， | Their bones are piled as high as Mt Meru,[2] |
| 别泪成海津。 | their farewell tears become a flooding sea. |
| 唯有空名在， | All that is left here is an empty name. |
| 岂免生死轮。 | The wheel of birth and death—where can one flee? |

## IV. Those keen on philosophy

| | |
|---|---|
| 我见利智人， | I look at those keen on philosophy, |
| 观著便如意。 | who comprehend all that they contemplate. |
| 不假寻文字， | Perusing written records ceaselessly, |
| 直入如来地。 | the Buddha-ground they easily penetrate. |
| 心不逐诸缘， | The mind is not attached to what it seeks, |
| 意根不妄起。 | and thus no wayward notions can arise. |
| 心意不生时， | When the sense of mind does not appear, |
| 内外无馀事。 | no excess things appear, inside, outside. |

**Notes**

1 *Old sage*: Zhuangzi or Chuang-tzu (c. 369-286 BCE) was a Daoist philosopher.

2 *Mt Meru*: sacred mountain, the axis of the world.

# Synkrētic
## SUBMISSIONS

Australia and its place in the world continue to evolve. Now more than ever, we have to understand our region and our place in it. *Synkrētic* is an outlet for thought-provoking writing on philosophy, literature and cultures, from and about the Indo-Pacific. It aims to showcase the diverse traditions of thought, story-telling and expression which are woven into the living tapestry of this culturally, linguistically and politically complex region. We're looking above all for well-written and substantive pieces for publication in the following formats.

| | |
|---:|:---|
| Essays | 3000 - 6000 words |
| Stories | ≤ 8000 words |
| Responses | 800 - 1600 words |
| Translations | ≤ 8000 words |
| Notes | 300 - 3000 words |

For details and guidelines:
**synkretic.com**

www.ingramcontent.com/pod-product-compliance
Lightning Source LLC
Chambersburg PA
CBHW020322010526
44107CB00054B/1938